DEBRETT'S
WEDDING
GUIDE

Debrett's Wedding Guide
Published by Debrett's Limited
18–20 Hill Rise, Richmond,
Surrey TW10 6UA
United Kingdom

Managing Editor
Jo Aitchison

Editor
Eleanor Mathieson

Editorial Assistants
Sarah Corney
Ellie Major

Concept and style Karen Wilks
Page design Design 23

**Additional editorial, index and
proof reading** Ruth Massey

Head of Publishing Elizabeth Wyse

Chairman Conrad Free

ISBN 978 1 870520 86 7

Printed and bound in Portugal by Avarto, Printer Portuguesa.

Visit us at www.debretts.co.uk

DEBRETT'S
WEDDING GUIDE

RACHEL MEDDOWES

Contents

Foreword

In the euphoric aftermath of announcing an engagement and the exciting early stages of planning, or helping to plan, a wedding, it isn't always easy to hang on to the real purpose behind it all — marriage. Yet marriage — the institution — doesn't at first sight seem to be in a particularly robust state. Most of us have only to think of our close circles of family and friends to realise that the formal arrangements by which couples and families traditionally ordered their lives are often forgone in favour of more flexible, 'modern' social structures.

Once upon a time, marriage, most particularly from a female point of view, was essential in order to function in society, let alone have any fun in life. Unmarried women, apart from a few redoubtable intellectuals, and those exorbitantly rich or confident and eccentric enough to carve out a path of their own, were doomed to a life devoid of most worldly satisfactions. They were usually beset by financial worries, had a poor social life and had to resign themselves not only to childlessness but also to a life without sex.

These days such a scenario seems almost laughable. Women are increasingly earning enough to give them economic freedom, if not actually earning more than men (in a significant number of 21st-century households the woman now does earn more than her man). A woman's social life is no longer dependent upon being married. It is quite possible to travel, or go to the theatre or a restaurant, on one's own, and groups of girls or women are perfectly capable of having a riotous time without a man in sight.

All these things must be considered benefits. Increasingly women are having children without the blessing of either clergy or a long-term partner, and society no longer regards this as anything to tut-tut about. Then, there is the happy fact that there is no longer any stigma attached to being gay. Unconventional arrangements abound.

It can sometimes seem as though society as we know it is coming apart at the seams, as if age-old patterns of organising ourselves and our families have been transformed beyond all recognition. But if we look a little deeper we see something else. We see that whilst the up-sides are there all right — economic freedom, greater honesty in relationships — we also find that more and more women are at least sensing that there is more to life than professional success and personal autonomy.

I well remember a meeting at which a group of highly successful women were sitting round the table. Someone mentioned that a former colleague had got married and moved to the country to be a mother of three. Envious gasps of 'Oh, wow …' abounded. It quickly became clear that many of those high-fliers would drop their current existences in a flash for the lure of family life: the farmhouse, the kids, the dogs in the back of the car …

Despite the career successes, the financial independence, many women still feel a deep longing for family life, the manifestation of an old biological need to bond: of one man committing to one woman and creating a safe haven for each other and their children. A longing too, as Sandy Boler, the ex-editor of *Brides* magazine, put it, 'to be safely gathered in' – something that marriage, in its best and most reassuring form, can do.

Which is possibly why I detect in the air, in the zeitgeist, something of a seismic backlash. Highly successful professional women earning salaries that resemble telephone numbers now seem to be indulging in what one commentator calls 'competitive breeding' – in other words creating and building very large families. What is interesting is that I don't believe that it's merely about the 'breeding'; I believe that it is part of a deeper urge, the urge to nest, to create the sort of family unit where

man, woman and their offspring can feel safe, where they are bound together by the most profound bonds of blood, love and kinship that no other institution can offer. There seems to be a yearning too for the sort of domestic dreams and certainties that were the norm some thirty or forty years ago but which these days have been replaced by dreams of breaking through glass ceilings and forging free and independent lives.

Those of us who are married know that it isn't easy. We know that long-lasting marriages, of forty, fifty, perhaps sixty years, have strains and stresses of their own, but it is hard to think of an institution that will do a better job of meeting our deepest human needs. De facto marriage, a serious commitment between man and woman, whether blessed by a priest or not, reaches far back into antiquity. It evolved because it was what men and women and their children needed if society was to be whole and sane.

The whole point of marriage is that the commitment that is made is significantly wider and broader than the simple promise two people make to each other – it is also the pact they make for the relationship itself, for their future children, and for the society in which they live. The institution isn't meant to be just a temporary deal that lasts for as long they both feel happy and in love – 'whatever that means', to use Prince Charles's famous phrase. It is an overarching institution that exists in almost every society, whether religious or pagan, for no one has yet come up with a better means of sheltering humankind from the things that life has to throw at us. It is more than just desirable. It is actually indispensable for the health and happiness not just of individuals but for society as a whole.

LUCIA VAN DER POST

FIRST THINGS FIRST

The Announcement

Announcing an engagement is a momentous step in a couple's life. The news will travel fast, so the essential consideration is not just how to disseminate it, but how to tell everyone at the right time.

Family should be prioritised, and the parents of both bride and groom should always be the very first to hear of an engagement. The groom may already have sought permission from the bride's father, so it may not come as such a surprise.

It is traditional for the man to ask his future father-in-law's permission for his daughter's hand in marriage, but it is often the case today that the couple get engaged and permission is sought, as a mere formality, afterwards. Gauge how traditional the family is and respect the expectations of the bride's father.

SPREADING THE NEWS

Telephone calls to the rest of the immediate family and close friends will follow; a round-robin email or text announcing the news is fine for everyone else. The traditional practice of sending a card announcing the engagement is less common nowadays.

Following that, the grapevine can be relied upon to spread the word. Consideration should be given to relatives and friends – it's best to avoid creating awkward situations by making as many calls as possible so people hear directly from the couple rather than by word-of-mouth.

The general reaction to the news may take the couple by surprise as they are flung into a social whirlwind, with friends clamouring to spend quality time with them. The couple are likely to want to celebrate with as many people as possible. Arranging an engagement party soon after the announcement, to which all friends can be invited, is a good idea.

FORMAL ANNOUNCEMENTS

Once the news has been spread by informal means, a formal announcement may be made in the local paper or a national broadsheet. It is traditional for the father of the bride to organise this where the bride's parents are hosting the wedding, or the couple may simply prefer to do it themselves.

A traditional announcement reads:

> Mr R Cooper and Miss K Fremantle
> The engagement is announced between Richard,
> elder son of Mr and Mrs John Cooper
> of Gask, Devon, and Kate, only daughter
> of Mr and Mrs Rufus Fremantle of Bayswater, London

If one or both sets of parents is divorced, the name and address of each parent is clearly spelt out:

> Mr R Cooper and Miss K Fremantle
> The engagement is announced between Richard,
> elder son of Mr John Cooper of Gask, Devon and
> Mrs Jane Cooper of Hammersmith, London, and Kate,
> only daughter of Mr Rufus Fremantle of Bayswater, London
> and Mrs Lily Coote of Helensburgh, Scotland

If a parent is widowed:

> Mr R Cooper and Miss K Fremantle
> The engagement is announced between Richard,
> elder son of Mr and Mrs John Cooper
> of Gask, Devon, and Kate, only daughter
> of Mrs Rufus Fremantle of Bayswater, London

A more contemporary style may be used:

> Mr Richard Cooper of Nant, Shropshire and Miss Kate Fremantle
> of Drem, East Lothian are delighted to announce their engagement.
> A summer wedding is planned

PARENTAL MEETINGS

It is traditional for the couple's parents to meet if they have not already done so once the announcement has been made.

The bride's mother traditionally writes to the groom's parents, expressing delight at the forthcoming marriage and suggesting that a date and venue be found for both sides to get together.

It is inappropriate to leave a first meeting to the engagement party, and highly inadvisable to leave it until the wedding day. If the parents do not already know each other, meeting in a neutral environment such as a restaurant may be a good idea, so that no one carries the burden of playing host or hostess.

The bride and groom should be there and every effort should be made to put both sets of parents at ease. Remember that first and foremost, this is a celebration. Any initial awkwardness is usually forgotten once the discussion of wedding plans is underway.

LETTERS AND PRESENTS

Congratulatory letters, notes, messages and presents will inevitably be sent by friends and family. Congratulations should always be conveyed in a handwritten letter; an email or text should be followed up by handwritten correspondence. In letters, it is traditional to congratulate the groom; it is considered impolite to congratulate the bride, as this implies that she has 'caught' her man. This rule is little known nowadays, so congratulating both is the norm.

It used to be considered desirable to send thank yous for presents by return post but convention has now relaxed; responding immediately is the polite thing to do, it is not absolutely imperative. Ideally, thanks should not be conveyed by email or text message.

The Rings

An engagement ring is a significant piece of jewellery. It is worn as a symbol of betrothal, although some brides will choose to wear only a wedding ring. Convention dictates that an engagement should be marked by a diamond ring, a practice that dates back to at least the eighteenth century. Other stones, such as sapphires and rubies, are still sometimes chosen for engagement rings, or may be used as side-settings.

It is still customary for the groom to pay for the ring. The rule that two months' salary should be spent on this has been relaxed. It is not necessary to present a ring when proposing; a safer option might be to give a piece of jewellery – such as a bracelet – that the groom knows his fiancée will like. However, the ring should be on her finger within a reasonable time.

The most important considerations are the bride's taste, her hand shape and her realistic expectations. If the groom is keen to have a say in the choice of ring, he may wish to select a few for his fiancée to choose from, or the couple may decide to look at rings together. A family heirloom – either a ring or a set of stones – may be donated by parents. This can be cleaned, adapted and re-set. If the bride is given a ring that is too valuable or precious to wear every day, she may wish to have a second ring that can be worn all the time.

If the couple choose the ring together, the budget should be established well in advance. Several styles should be tried, perhaps in various shops. It is advisable to experiment with a range of cuts, sizes and settings.

Trusted or recommended jewellers should be used. It is very easy to be talked into buying stones without knowing what they are really worth: an enormous diamond is not necessarily more valuable than a smaller, well cut, flawless stone, and a discreet ring may be more suited to everyday wear.

DIAMONDS

Retailers will be happy to advise on the quality of stones. A diamond will be valued using the 'Four Cs':

✸ Cut: its shape and how well it has been cut to that shape (common cuts include brilliant, oval, princess, marquise, emerald and pear).

✸ Clarity: the measure of its purity and the number of natural blemishes ('inclusions') the diamond carries.

✸ Colour: how tinted the diamond looks. There is a scale from D to Z, with D being the clearest and most expensive.

✸ Carat: the measure of the stone's weight. One carat is 200 milligrams (the weight of a small paperclip) and there are 100 points to a carat.

THE WEDDING RINGS

Choosing a wedding band that complements the engagement ring, and vice versa, is of course a major consideration for the bride – the two rings must look good together, and be comfortable. It is worth trying the engagement ring on with wedding bands to see how they sit together on the hand, since the engagement ring will look different alongside another ring, rather than on a plain finger.

There are three ring shapes to choose from: D (curved edge), flat (straight edge) and court (tapered edge).

The engagement and wedding rings should be made of the same metal, otherwise over time the stronger metal will wear away the weaker one. The most popular metals for wedding bands are:

Gold: which comes in a vast range of shades, tones and carats. White gold may 'yellow' over time and will need to be re-plated every ten years.

Platinum: an expensive option, but it will never need to be re-plated.

Titanium: incredibly durable yet lightweight.

Many brides choose to wear eternity rings, or patterned and engraved rings, instead of a plain band. Those who prefer to wear silver jewellery should consider white gold or platinum.

In terms of style, the general rule for both men and women is the wider the hand, the thicker the band should be. Several rings should be tried.

Whilst it used to be uncommon for men to wear wedding rings, this is now very much accepted practice. Traditionally, the groom's ring is paid for by the bride.

OTHER CONSIDERATIONS

An engraved message or date inside the band adds a bespoke touch.

The perfect fit will incorporate a small amount of leeway for swelling (allow enough space for a cocktail stick to slide in and out easily).

Both the wedding rings and the engagement ring represent a major outlay, and therefore must be insured – the latter to the full value of the stone or stones. Jewellers' receipts should be kept in a safe place in case a claim has to be made.

Many brides-to-be like to give a substantial present to their fiancé, as a way of marking the significance of the occasion. Popular choices include, a watch, cufflinks, or a beautiful pen.

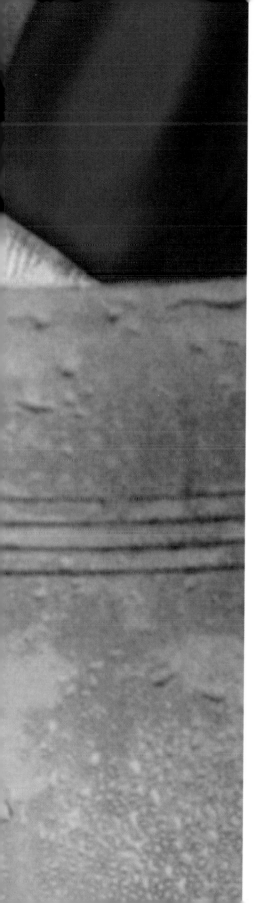

Engagement Parties

The engagement party is by no means an essential step on the road to marriage, but it is a great excuse for a celebratory gathering. Inevitably, friends and family will be keen to see the couple in person to offer their congratulations.

It may also be the first time many guests meet either the bride or groom and their respective friends and family. Introductions made at the engagement party will be invaluable come the wedding itself, relieving the hosts of pressure to ensure that guests are mingling.

Ideally, the party should be held within a month or two of announcing the engagement. One set of parents may choose to organise the party, in which case it is customary for the father of the bride to give a small speech and toast the couple. Alternatively, the couple may wish to host the party themselves. Sometimes it might be appropriate to hold two parties – one for families and family friends, and a more relaxed occasion for the couple's friends.

The primary host should send out the invitations, always checking before setting a date that key guests will be able to attend. It should be clearly noted on invitations that the party is being held to mark the engagement.

Obviously, the scale and lavishness of the party will be dictated by budget. Finances permitting, champagne and canapés are a fail-safe formula for this type of party.

CONSIDERATIONS

A cautionary note: guests invited to the engagement party will expect to be invited to the wedding too.

Presents for the engaged couple should be acknowledged with a thank you letter. Guests should write a thank you letter to the host after the event.

Money Management

Money doesn't have to be a tense subject, so long as discussions happen at an early date and in an open fashion. A realistic budget should be decided upon at the outset, and frank discussion is therefore imperative. It may burst the bubble of excitement, but an early decision on the budget will smooth the planning stages. Once the budget is set, negotiations can start.

A first step may be for the couple to have a discussion with their parents. Traditionally, the bride's father bears the cost, but this is by no means expected today; parents on both sides may be keen to help out. If the in-laws do not contribute towards the wedding, they may wish to host a pre- or post-wedding dinner or lunch.

Alternatively, the couple may wish to pay for the entire day themselves. As couples nowadays often marry later in life, and both men and women enjoy financial independence, the old norms aren't always applicable.

Whatever the financial situation, just because someone is contributing towards the wedding does not mean that they control it. This is tricky ground – open discussion before accepting generous parental donations may save a lot of trouble further down the line.

CLEVER BUDGETING

By recording all estimated and real costs, an overall picture of expenditure levels can be monitored – most couples change their minds several times as to exactly what they want and how much they are willing to allocate to any given aspect, so a concrete budget right at the beginning is unrealistic.

Everyone involved in planning the wedding will have different ideas about spending priorities. This is an area where the generation gap often shows, so exercising a little understanding and patience is advisable. Involve as few people as possible, set a budget and work towards it.

BUDGET PRIORITIES

There are two key mantras that should be borne in mind at all times: prioritise and compromise. Think about what is essential, what is unnecessary and the areas where costs can be cut. Be assured that however much the budget is, it will never be enough, so even those with large amounts of money to spend will be restricted. Costs should never be underestimated.

It is a good idea to identify the most important elements of the day at the outset, for example: the reception venue, the dress and the quality of the wine. Ensuring there is a constant flow of wine and investing in great entertainment might be considered far more crucial than investing in thousands of pounds' worth of flowers to decorate the venue.

Elaborate food will make a dent in even the most generous budgets but as a bad dinner will be something that guests remember, the answer may be to choose quality over quantity. For example, a delicious simple main course and pudding will be much more enjoyable than a mediocre five-course lunch.

PREPARING THE PROVISIONAL BUDGET

First, agree on a total provisional cost. Where parents are contributing, their input should be taken into account.

Next, the time-consuming research needs to be done: shop around and record the estimated amount to be allocated to each feature of the wedding.

FINALISING THE BUDGET

As costs are finalised, a record should be kept of the total sum plus any deposit paid. Now it is simply a matter of balancing the books. When a saving is made, the amount saved can be allocated to a different area, and likewise where the budget is exceeded, a saving must be made in another area, or extra cash found.

QUOTATIONS AND COSTS

Most suppliers of services will provide the customer with an estimate for their services. It is vitally important to note the difference between an estimate (just that) and a quotation (the real amount to be paid, which is set in stone). The final budget should, of course, be prepared only after acquiring quotations, rather than relying on estimates that may no longer reflect the extent of the service being provided.

A large event such as a wedding requires careful organisation; chaotic paperwork will only add to pre-wedding stress. All correspondence, quotations and receipts should be kept, and a note made of deposits paid, when balances are due, and sums outstanding. Be aware that most suppliers' quotes exclude VAT, so allow for the extra percentage to be added on.

THE 'W' WORD

Any goods or services associated with the word 'wedding' will automatically be marked up in price. Ways of achieving the same result without falling into this trap – perhaps using friends, acquaintances, or personal recommendations – should be investigated. Areas where it might be possible to bypass the big wedding suppliers are the cake, bridesmaids' dresses and flowers.

TIPPING

Tips are not usually made to companies or individuals that supply services at 'wedding rates'. Friends or acquaintances who give special rates – for example a florist who supplies the flowers at cost and does the arranging for free – may be better rewarded with a thoughtful present rather than the host insisting on paying market rates.

Equally, friends who go beyond the call of duty for the wedding day deserve a thank you present. Costs add up, so these extra add-ons must not be forgotten.

Who Pays for What?

Here is a checklist of elements of the day, along with an indication of who traditionally pays. Modern weddings are normally a variation on these traditions. **B**=bride; **BF**=bride's family and **G**=groom.

ATTIRE

Wedding dress, veil, shoes, lingerie and jewellery **BF**
Bridesmaids' dresses, pageboy outfits and accessories **BF**
Something old, new, borrowed and blue **B**
Groom's outfit **G**
Best man's outfit **G** or **best man**
Ushers' outfits **G** or **ushers**
Groom's going-away outfit **G**
Bride's going-away outfit **B**

BRIDAL BEAUTY

Hairdressing and make-up **B**

TRANSPORTATION

To ceremony: bride, bride's father, bridesmaids and bride's mother **BF**
Ceremony to reception: bride and groom **BF**
Decorations (ribbons) for wedding transportation **BF**
To ceremony: groom and best man **G**
From reception: bride and groom **G**

PHOTOGRAPHY

Photography or videoing **BF**

FLOWERS

Church **BF**
Reception **BF**
Bride's and bridesmaids' bouquets **BF** or **G**
Buttonholes **BF or G**

CEREMONY

Civil/religious ceremony fees **G**
Church, plus extras (bells, organist, choir) **G**
Register office or other venue fees **G**

RECEPTION

Venue hire and decorations **BF**
Toastmaster **BF**
Wedding cake **BF**
Catering **BF**
Favours **BF**
Drinks **BF**
Entertainment **BF**

HONEYMOON

Passports and visas **G**
Travel and accommodation **G**
Bride's clothing **B**
Groom's clothing **G**
Spending money **G**
Travel insurance and inoculations **G**

STATIONERY

Invitations and postage **BF**
Order of Service **BF**
Menus and place name cards **BF**
Seating plan chart **BF**

PRESENTS

Bride's engagement and wedding rings **G**
Groom's wedding ring **B**
Presents for bridesmaids, ushers and best man **G**
Presents for bride and groom's parents **B** and **G**

OTHER

Engagement party **BF**
Wedding planner fees **BF**
Wedding insurance **BF**
Press announcements for engagement **BF**
Press announcements for wedding **G**
Wedding night hotel **G**
Overnight accommodation for close family **BF**
Note: the cost of stag and hen parties are generally shared among those who attend

Pre-Nuptials and Insurance

A pre-nuptial agreement is a contract entered into by a couple before marriage, which aims to clarify how their assets will be divided in the event of divorce.

LEGALITIES

Pre-nuptial agreements are not currently legally binding in the UK and cannot be enforced in the divorce courts. However, they may be taken into account, and judges are increasingly prepared to respect them.

PROS

There are many ways in which such a contract can be useful. It gives each person the chance to record their assets as they stand before the marriage, using this information to decide on a fair division of assets should the marriage break down.

It can also help a couple if, for example, they come from different countries or religious backgrounds and want to establish precisely what kind of religious education they are going to choose for their children.

CONS

There are a number of issues with such a contract. Intervening time is a factor: the financial circumstances of one or both parties may change between the time the pre-nuptial agreement is drawn up and the time the marriage breaks down.

There may also be children to take into account. The tradition of the English divorce courts is to ensure that assets are divided fairly, with consideration of the apparent needs of the parties and of any children. If there are children, their needs will always be seen as more important than adhering to a pre-nuptial agreement.

THE FUTURE

The law relating to pre-nuptial agreements is changing and there are calls to make them legally binding.

WEDDING INSURANCE

Weddings involve a substantial outlay, and insurance is one of the first priorities when planning the wedding. It should be put in place as soon as the budget is established and before the couple begin to book suppliers, as it covers against such issues as cancellations, failure of suppliers, accidents, problems with the wedding transport and loss of the rings.

Wedding insurance can be purchased from banks and high street stores as well as specialist insurance companies, so it is wise to research all options and the cover they offer.

BASIC COVER

There are various levels of wedding insurance, but the following will usually be covered:

✳ Accidental injury to any person.

✳ Cancellation of the wedding or reception.

✳ Loss of, or damage to, the wedding attire for the main wedding party.

✳ Loss of, or damage to, the wedding rings, cake, flowers or presents.

✳ Failure of any supplier.

✳ Failure of prints and videos.

✳ Failure of wedding cars and transport.

✳ Legal expenses.

The insurance policy will not cover cancellation costs if either the bride or groom decides not to go through with the wedding.

The Guest List

By the time the engaged couple are ready to draw up the guest list, they may already have attended dozens of friends' weddings and parties. The process of choosing guests, however, is not about returning favours. The couple must actively want their guests to be there, and anyone whose friendship has lapsed, or who might attend with anything but the very best of sentiments, should be considered with caution. Familial repercussions must be borne in mind where family members are concerned.

PRACTICALITIES

Traditionally, the bride's mother sends out the invitations, but the couple may choose to take on that responsibility themselves.

A certain number of invitations should be allocated to each set of parents. The person financing the majority of the wedding may try to insist on having more influence, but if satisfactory discussions took place and were resolved at an early stage, this situation should not arise.

The budget and venue size will determine the number of guests. If the church or register office (or other venue) is small, it is acceptable to invite some guests to the reception alone, or just to evening celebrations.

Under no circumstances should a guest be invited to the wedding but not to the reception.

Courtesy invitations should be sent out to guests who the host knows will be unable to attend due to illness or great distance.

The best man, all bridesmaids and pages and the couple's parents (except the parents who are doing the inviting) should receive a formal invitation as a matter of courtesy. If the person conducting the wedding ceremony is to attend the reception, he or she should also be on the list.

COMPILING AND MANAGING THE LIST

A draft wish list should be compiled, listing every possible person. This is shaved down until a realistic number of guests has been settled on. Ensure that a record of names of those who did not make the final count is maintained; this is the reserve guest list.

Family should come first. In instances where either the bride or the groom has a considerably larger family than their partner an equal split may not be possible. If both families are large, the number of friends on the guest list may have to be reduced.

A record of those invited should be kept – responses can be recorded on this list as they come in. When refusals are received, invitations can be sent to those on the reserve guest list. Dispatching a second wave of invitations is quite acceptable, so long as they are not sent out way after the original invitations. If there is a long delay, the reserve guests may become aware that they were not first choices.

At some point a policy decision will have to be made on whether all partners of guests should be invited. There is no generally accepted rule, but if the guest is married or in an established, long-term relationship, his or her spouse/partner should be invited. Otherwise, if the couple has not met the partner of the guest in question, it is usually acceptable not to invite them.

Note that, when inviting partners, the use of the words 'and guest' after a guest's name should be avoided if at all possible – try to establish names, including surnames.

GUEST ETIQUETTE

If an invitation has not been received, it is considered the height of rudeness to ask for one. If an invitation has arrived and it does not specify 'and guest', it is equally rude to ask to bring one.

Setting the Date

There are no fixed traditions, but a minimum of six months is usually required to plan a wedding.

It can take up to twelve months, particularly if the couple want to book a popular church or reception venue where there will probably be only a limited number of slots available, especially at busy times.

If the ceremony is to be held at a register office or the home of the bride/groom, there will be more leeway and things will take less time to organise. It is quite unusual for an engagement to last more than 18 months.

Couples who set the date over a year in advance can find that this long a waiting period can increase both stress levels and impatience.

THE COUPLE'S CHOICE

The day and time are dependent on many factors; the first decision to be made is the time of year. The bride may always have dreamt of getting married by candlelight in winter, in an informal sundress in the garden at her parents' home, which will work best in July, or on a beach on the west coast of Mexico in November. Equally the choice of wedding day may be a good opportunity to mark a significant anniversary.

Spring and summer, from May to September, are still the most popular months in England, with June being the busiest of all. The planning of the honeymoon should also be taken into consideration at this point — is the dream destination suitable at that time of year? Can both bride and groom take time off work then?

LIMITING FACTORS

Once potential dates have been agreed, the most sensible thing to do next is check the availability of members of the wedding party and opt for the date that produces the best result.

Pinning everyone down to a single date will be virtually impossible, so compromises will have to be made. Ideally, the day should not clash with major sporting events or bank holidays, and school and summer holidays should be considered – choosing an August wedding, when many friends may be abroad, might cut down the chances of the most valued guests attending. Equally, a Christmas wedding may clash with too many guests' family commitments.

Saturday is the most popular day for weddings, simply because it is a weekend day. Fridays may prove to be a good alternative where a Saturday isn't available, since many guests will welcome the opportunity of a long weekend – this may be better than having to wait another six months for the next available Saturday.

SECURING THE VENUE

Finalising the date essentially involves a process of elimination. The availability of venues on certain dates is the next factor that comes into play. If the ceremony is to be religious, a separate reception venue will need to be booked; for many civil ceremonies held in approved venues (hotels, castles, etc.), the ceremony and reception can often take place in the same building, simplifying the booking process.

If two venues are required, the venue for the ceremony should be firmed up first; then, when looking at reception venues, it will often be possible to pencil the date in with various places, especially if this is done well in advance. This will allow for a little more time to be taken over this all-important decision.

Finding ideal locations is far harder than anyone ever believes, but it is worth persisting and pursuing all options until one is found that meets the majority of the criteria. Once the decision has been made, deposits should be paid immediately to secure the venue(s).

Stationery Basics

The first hint of the style of the wedding, be it traditional, contemporary or innovative, is revealed the moment the invitation lands on a guest's doormat.

The most traditional and elegant wedding invitations combine quality of material with simplicity of style. Many consider customised, engraved stationery a good investment, although online services are an option for more limited budgets.

SUGGESTED STATIONERY

* Save the date cards (optional): sent to ask guests to keep the day free. The wording should be kept brief, such as:

Please Save the Date

For the marriage of

Richard Cooper and Kate Fremantle

Saturday 10th June 2008

London

Invitation to follow

* Invitation: sent out 10–12 weeks in advance of the day, (and evening invitations, if applicable).

* Reply cards (optional): small pre-printed single cards, supplied with a stamped addressed envelope, for RSVP.

* Order of service/ceremony: containing the outline of the ceremony, with the words of hymns or songs printed in full, details of readings, and the readers' names.

* Thank you cards (optional): to be sent to guests to thank them for their wedding presents.

* Place name cards (these can be hand-made and handwritten): for the tables at the reception.

* Menu: listing food and wines at the reception.

CHOOSING THE STYLE

Some basic factors will dictate the look and feel of the invitation: size and shape, colour, material and typeface. Finishing touches (a lined envelope and ribbons), and possibly an additional 'device', for example a personalised monogram that can be used on all the wedding stationery, will make a real impact.

Traditional wedding stationery, with its distinctive copperplate script, has a very inflexible format, but there is nothing to say that more contemporary styles and wording cannot be used – there are no set rules. The couple may introduce a theme, be it vintage, retro, or minimalist, which will reflect the general look and feel of the wedding. Invitations can include photographs or illustrations, blind embossing, motifs or monograms. They may also be printed on unusual materials, such as vinyl, perspex, leaves or fabric.

ORDERING

Stationery orders should include plenty of spares to allow for mistakes when writing on them, and enough to send out a second batch once refusals have come in – reprints will be extremely expensive.

It is generally estimated that around 20 per cent of invitations are refused, but this cannot be relied upon in the planning stages. Beware of over-ordering: a common mistake is to order an invitation for each guest, forgetting that many will be couples who will receive a joint invitation.

Once all the details have been finalised, a proof will be sent to the couple for approval. The proof should be checked extremely carefully, particularly dates and the spellings of names. At least four weeks should be allowed from the time the order is made to receiving the printed stationery, more if the stationery is to be printed in spring ahead of the busy summer months.

Invitations: Correct Form

A traditional wedding invitation is made of heavy card. It should be 8 x 6 inches (20.3 x 15.2 cm) folded in half with the text on the first (outer) page. This is usually in black copperplate script, on a cream or white matt background.

The name of the guest is handwritten in ink in the top left-hand corner. A calligrapher can be hired to address the invitations and envelopes.

On formal invitations, guests should be addressed by their full title, for example, Mr and Mrs Aaron Williams, Miss Eleanor Copcutt, the Lady Alice Torstenson. For less formal invitations it is acceptable to use only first names.

The traditional format for a wedding invitation where both parents are married is as follows:

Mr and Mrs John Standish
request the pleasure of
your company at the marriage
of their daughter
Caroline
to
Mr Christopher John Herbert
at St Paul's Church, Knightsbridge
on Saturday 15th March 2008
at 3 o'clock
and afterwards at
The Hyde Park Hotel, London SW1

The RSVP address is then included in the bottom left hand corner of the invitation.

Many families, however, will not fit into this pattern; there are a number of alternative styles of wording for different circumstances.
Note: the bride and groom's middle names may also be included.

If the bride's mother is the hostess:

Mrs John Standish
requests the pleasure of
your company at the marriage
of her daughter
Caroline

If the bride's father is the host:

Mr John Standish
requests the pleasure of
your company at the marriage
of his daughter
Caroline

If the bride's mother and stepfather are the joint host/hostess:

Mr and Mrs Edgar Forsythe
request the pleasure of
your company at the marriage
of her daughter
Caroline Standish

If the bride's father and her stepmother are the joint host/hostess:

Mr and Mrs John Standish
request the pleasure of
your company at the marriage
of his daughter
Caroline

Where the bride's stepmother is the hostess:

Mrs John Standish
requests the pleasure of
your company at the marriage
of her stepdaughter
Caroline

If the bride's parents are divorced, but are nevertheless co-hosting the wedding:

Mr John Standish and Mrs Edgar Forsythe*
request the pleasure of
your company at the marriage
of their daughter
Caroline

* 'Mrs Jane Standish' if she has not remarried

If the hosts are the bride's relatives, guardians or godparents are host/hostess:

Mr and Mrs Robert Newton
request the pleasure of
your company at the marriage
of their ward Caroline Standish*

* The bride's surname may be included if it is different to the host's/hostess's

If the bride is the hostess:

Miss Caroline Standish
requests the pleasure of your company
at her marriage to
Mr Christopher Herbert

Where the bride and groom are the host and hostess:

Mr Christopher Herbert and Miss Caroline Standish
request the pleasure of
your company at their marriage

In certain circumstances an invitation may be sent to the reception only – the same rules relating to the naming of the hosts will apply:

Mr and Mrs James Burton
request the pleasure of
your company at the reception following the marriage
of their daughter
Beatrice Jane

A note should be placed inside the envelope with the invitation to give a good reason, for example:
Owing to the small size of St John's Church it is possible to ask only very few guests to the service. We hope you will forgive this invitation being to the reception only.

SECOND AND SUBSEQUENT MARRIAGES

In the case of a divorced bride embarking on a second marriage, whichever example above is applicable to the bride should be used. If the bride's marriage has been dissolved, she is described as 'Mrs Catriona Short'. If she has reverted to her maiden name, it is only necessary to list her forename, as in the standard invitations above.

If the bride is the hostess, the examples above should be followed, with her name as 'Mrs Joseph Short' or 'Mrs Catriona Short', as applicable. If the bride is a widow, she is described as 'Catriona, widow of Mr Joseph Short'.

Information, Replies, Cancellations

FURTHER INFORMATION

A separate sheet giving practical information can be included with the invitation; it is fine to print these at home, as long as a good printer and quality paper are used. The following information typically appears within these enclosures:

Directions to both the church/venue and reception, plus a map and details of local train stations and airports. Never assume that guests know their way around.

Accommodation details – local hotels and B&Bs covering all price ranges – plus local taxi firms. Where the evening reception is to be held in a hotel, reduced rates should have been negotiated.

If no reference is made to dress code on a formal invitation, then morning attire should be worn. Black tie or suits should be specifically mentioned.

Policy on children.

Details of where the wedding list is held, with website, address and phone number (while traditionalists still maintain that reference to the wedding list should not be included with the invitation, it is almost universal practice to enclose such information, and eyebrows are generally not raised these days).

A request to inform the host of special dietary requirements or allergies when accepting the invitation.

The time the events will draw to a close – often referred to as 'carriages'.

Contact number of the host(s) in case of questions.

The date by which guests should reply, usually two months before the day.

REPLIES

Replies should be handwritten, in the third person, on headed paper. The envelope is addressed to the hostess and the date should written at the bottom of the page. For example:

Mr and Mrs David Clegg thank Mr and Mrs John Standish for the kind invitation to the marriage of their daughter, Caroline, to Mr Christopher John Herbert at St Paul's, Knightsbridge, on Saturday 15th March at 3 o'clock and afterwards at The Hyde Park Hotel, and are delighted to accept/regret that they are unable to accept.

POSTPONEMENTS AND CANCELLATIONS

If a wedding is postponed due to unforeseen circumstances, or cancelled, a white or cream card, measuring 5.5 x 3.5 inches (14 x 9 cm), is sent out. The following wording is recommended:

Indefinite postponement:
Owing to the recent death of Mr Samuel Herbert, Mr and Mrs John Standish deeply regret that they are obliged to cancel the invitations to the marriage of their daughter Caroline to Mr Christopher John Herbert on...

Postponement to a later date:
Owing to the illness of Mrs Sheila Herbert, Mr and Mrs John Standish deeply regret that they are obliged to postpone the invitations to the marriage of their daughter Caroline to Mr Christopher John Herbert at St Paul's, Knightsbridge from Saturday, 15 March 2008 to Thursday, 9 May 2008

If the wedding is to take place quietly:
Owing to the recent death of her husband, Mrs John Standish much regrets that she is obliged to cancel the invitations to the marriage of her daughter Caroline to Mr Christopher John Herbert, which will now take place very quietly on Thursday, 9 May 2008

If the engagement is broken off:
Mr and Mrs John Standish announce that the marriage of their daughter Caroline to Mr Christopher John Herbert, which was arranged for Saturday, 15 March 2008, will not take place

Forms of Address

Graham Barlow is a medical doctor. This form of address applies even if the wife is a medical doctor: Dr and Mrs Graham Barlow (invitation), Mrs Graham Barlow (envelope).

Single man: Mr Mark Barlow (invitation), Mark Barlow, Esq (envelope).

Single woman: Miss Miriam Barlow (invitation), Miss Miriam Barlow (envelope).

Widowed woman: Mrs Graham Barlow (invitation), Mrs Graham Barlow (on the envelope).

Divorced woman: Mrs Janet Barlow (invitation), Mrs Janet Barlow (envelope).

Unmarried couple in an established relationship: Miss Miriam Barlow and Mr Patrick Grant (invitation), Miss Miriam Barlow and Patrick Grant, Esq (envelope).

Same sex partner in an established relationship: Mr Edgar Wall and Mr Jon Bates (invitation), Edgar Wall, Esq and Jon Bates, Esq (envelope).

Single man and guest where the guest is not known well: Mr Mark Barlow and Miss Jane Hughes (invitation), Mark Barlow, Esq (envelope).

Single woman and guest where the guest is not known well: Miss Miriam Barlow and Mr Philip Wright (on the invitation), Miss Miriam Barlow (envelope).

Church of England vicar where the spouse is not known well: Reverend and Mrs Anthony Lambert (invitation), The Reverend Anthony Lambert (envelope).

Roman Catholic priest: Father Lambert (invitation), The Reverend Father Lambert (envelope).

FORMS OF ADDRESS

It is important to style guests correctly on both the invitation and the envelope, and there are a number of guidelines to follow. Here are some useful, and commonly used, forms of address:

Married couple where both are well known: Mr and Mrs Graham Barlow (invitation), Mrs Graham Barlow (envelope). Omitting children's names excludes them from the invitation.

Married couple with invited children: Mr and Mrs Graham Barlow, Adam and Claire (invitation), Mrs Graham Barlow (envelope).

Married couple where only the husband is known well, for example a male work colleague: Mr and Mrs Graham Barlow (invitation), Graham Barlow, Esq (envelope).

FUNDAMENTALS

Tone and Style of the Day

Traditional, modern, romantic, vintage or retro, the options for the style of the wedding day are numerous. Once a budget has been allocated, the bride and groom must decide what type of wedding they want.

CEREMONY

The first choice to be made is between a religious and a civil ceremony. With the latter, there is a further choice between a register office and an approved venue (such as a stately home or hotel), which has a bearing on whether a separate reception location will need to be booked.

SEASON

The time of year is very important, as the seasons dictate the tone and certain practicalities of the day, including dress, weather, food and flowers.

LOCATION

The location dictates elements of style. A city wedding may require more sophistication than a rural setting; a marquee in a country garden is very different from the formality of a hotel. The bride and groom should choose a theme that fits the venue's surroundings and style.

NUMBERS

The number of guests and level of formality should be established early on – this may affect the choice and style of reception venue; for example, a smaller venue may be required for an afternoon reception with canapés, whereas more room is needed for a full sit-down dinner. There will be different priorities and considerations for an intimate day with under 100 guests than for a large wedding catering for, say, 175 people.

COLOUR

Colour is a useful tool in creating a theme. The simplest, and most successful, combination comprises three elements: first, white or ivory; secondly, gold or silver; and finally a colour, for example pink. This combination can then be reflected throughout the day.

Often, the bridesmaids will coordinate with the chosen colour. The bouquets and flower arrangements should also pick it up, as should details such as ribbons, candles, napkins and favours.

CONSISTENCY

All style decisions must reflect the tone of the wedding. If a country wedding is decided upon, for example, then all elements of the day must be considered in this light, from beginning to end.

PERSONAL TOUCH

Personal home-made touches can make the wedding day unique. If a family member or close friend is an excellent cake maker, musician or florist, use their skills, so long as they are willing. Friends love to be involved, but the bride and groom should ensure that they don't put anyone in an awkward position, or that anyone is out of pocket. Reassure friends that their help is being sought with the aim of making the day personal, rather than as a way of saving money.

BUDGET

The date and time of a wedding can have a major impact on the budget. Choosing to marry on a weekday at a quiet time of year often means that venue costs can be kept to a minimum.

Many couples approach their wedding planning with grand ideas and are unaware how quickly the budget can escalate. They must be prepared to compromise and reassess their options at each stage. By choosing a style and theme for their wedding, they can frequently revisit their expectations and have a joint vision of how the day will look and feel. It is then easier to fill in the gaps and plan the day in full, rather than feeling unfocused with a budget that is spiralling out of control.

Wedding List

The circumstances and age of the bride and groom often influence the choice of wedding list and presents. A young couple setting up home will have clear priorities, which will be very different to the expectations of an older, established couple.

SETTING UP A LIST

Lists are available through department stores, specialist wedding list companies, independent shops or even charities. The list must be set up at least three months in advance and before the invitations go out.

For busy couples, there are online or web-based services that can help them to manage the list and make amendments at any time, even after the wedding itself. These are convenient for couples who aren't able to dedicate time to wedding list shopping (choosing items for the wedding list in-store).

COMPILING A LIST

The bride and groom should choose items across a wide price range, which will help to make guests feel less restricted in their choice of present. Couples whose homes are well equipped can choose presents that are more specialised. More unusual options include donations to charity (an increasingly popular green option), building on a collection of books or furniture, or starting a wine cellar. It is unusual to ask for money; some couples simply request nothing at all.

Once the items have been chosen and the list compiled, the holding company will manage the list on behalf of the couple. Guests will be able to buy in-store, online or over the phone.

The bride and groom will be kept up to date with purchases and informed if the list needs topping up. The list-holder will also store the goods until it is convenient for the bride and groom to receive them, usually after the honeymoon.

INFORMING GUESTS

Traditionally, guests contacted the bride's mother to find out where the list was being held, but nowadays most couples include details of the wedding list in the information pack that is sent with the invitations. Alternatively, details can be sent out after acceptances arrive. This may not be practical, however, as many guests who are unable to attend still like to give a present.

ON OR OFF THE LIST?

Guests should not think that they are being unoriginal by buying from the list. After all, the couple have specifically requested those items and a wedding list is often a one-off opportunity to receive certain luxuries. However, a guest is free to do something different if they would like to give a unique or individual present. They must be sure of the couple's taste before taking this step.

Wedding Planners

A wedding planner is a good option for a busy bride and groom, or for a couple who have a generous budget but are uncertain as to exactly what they want.

PROJECT MANAGEMENT

Most couples underestimate the time it takes to plan a wedding, the practicalities involved and the vast number of options available. The wedding planner is there to project manage, coordinate meetings with suppliers and secure bookings. They will also be present on the day.

A bride and groom who are considering hiring a wedding planner should remember that their function is to advise and organise, rather than dictate and take over. A good planner should take the couple's expectations and visions of the big day and translate them into reality.

CHOOSING AND HIRING

Where possible, the bride and groom should follow personal recommendation and interview several different planners to see whose manner and outlook best matches their expectations. If the parents are paying, their opinion should also be sought.

A good planner will be adept at working to a budget, managing tricky family situations, dealing with crises and brokering deals. Above all, they will be flexible.

COMMUNICATION

Once the planner is on board, they will attend all supplier meetings. It is a good idea to nominate one person – usually the bride – as the planner's point of contact to avoid any breakdown in communication.

The planner will involve the couple at every stage of the process, talk through ideas and develop the couple's vision for the big day.

SUPPLIERS

A wedding planner's unique value lies in their contacts. These are of paramount importance, and would otherwise be hard to come by. The planner is armed with a choice of highly regarded and trusted suppliers such as florists, caterers, photographers, set builders, musicians and staff. Moreover, a wedding planner will have an established relationship with suppliers and will be able to secure discounts and favours. The discounts that they can secure from the suppliers in their little black book will go some way towards compensating for the cost of a planner.

PART TIME PLANNERS

If the wedding budget does not stretch to include a planner's fee, or if the couple wish to do some of the organising themselves, some planners can be employed just to take care of certain elements of the day, or give general advice, charged by the hour.

SUPPORT

A wedding planner will be on constant call for any panics, concerns or worries. If the bride has a very demanding job, it is essential that she can call and rely upon her wedding planner for practical, and sometimes emotional, support. On such a momentous occasion emotions run high, and it is quite likely that the bride, groom and other close family members will become good friends with the wedding planner and enjoy sharing the euphoria of the day.

FEES

A deposit is required in advance. Most wedding planners charge a percentage – approximately 10–15 per cent – of the total cost of the wedding, with a minimum charge. This floating arrangement can feel financially daunting. If a planner is prepared to work for a fixed fee, this is the preferable option as it allows the couple to make an exact provision in the wedding budget, but it is a less common form of payment. In either case, terms and conditions should be given in writing before the bride and groom consent to anything.

Photography

Photographs are a unique and valuable record of the big day, so photography is an area where money is usually well spent. Specialist wedding photographers are not essential; many couples choose a professional with experience. Personal recommendations are often best, but the couple should do their research and work out what they want. It is worth investing in a professional; relying on friends can be risky. While they may take some of the most natural and memorable pictures on the day, the couple need someone fully dedicated to the task.

STYLE

The bride and groom will decide on the style they want. Reportage – or 'fly-on-the-wall' – is a natural and more interesting option than the traditional posed, formal shots. Ideally, the photographer should be able to do both, providing a vivid record of the day along with selected formal shots. The couple also need to decide whether they want black and white or colour images, or a selection of both.

MAKING A CHOICE

Many photographers keep portfolios of selected shots from a variety of weddings, but to ensure that they are of a consistent standard, the bride and groom should request to see a whole set from just one wedding. View pictures as prints, not just online.

Check at the outset whether the photographer works with film or uses a digital camera. Nowadays, many couples like to upload photos online for guests to access. If the photographer works with film it can be costly and time-consuming to upload photos, since each print will have to be individually scanned.

BACKUP

Check the small print to ensure that the photographer has proper insurance and a backup plan in case they fall ill or have an equipment failure.

COSTS

Pricing is usually based on the length of time the photographer is required, how many pictures the couple want and how they would like them presented. Some top end packages offer a photographer for the entire day, arriving early to capture the bride getting ready and staying until the guests leave the reception. They may also include an assistant or second photographer.

A standard package offers one photographer, who begins by taking shots at the ceremony, and stays until the first dance. If extra photography is required, overtime will be charged at an hourly rate, which is often very expensive.

Often photographers also charge for travel and accommodation costs. A deposit – usually 25 per cent – will be required upon booking to secure the date, with the balance payable on delivery of the pictures.

THE FINAL CUT

The couple will be offered a range of albums of varying sizes and quality to choose from, or they may opt to choose their own. The prints will be numbered up in the album so that the bride and groom can easily identify which ones they would like to re-order.

On average, the bride and groom will choose anywhere from 200–600 photos, depending on the agreed package. Quite often the package will include a set number of photos. The couple will then be charged for each extra photo chosen. This set-up can prove very advantageous to the photographer.

It is worth considering buying the copyright for the photographs at the outset. The couple can then pick and choose to print as many photographs as they wish. Most couples end up with an album of up to 150 photos.

CONSIDERATIONS AND PLANNING

✳ It is sensible to ask for a set of engagement photos to be taken. This is a good test of the quality of the photography, and will establish whether the photographer has the ability to put people at ease.

✳ It is essential that the photographer does a site visit before the ceremony in order to familiarise themselves with the layout and location of the venue.

✳ The photographer should be fully briefed about any special requirements or unusual situations. They must be aware of how the day is structured, and where they need to be at what time.

✳ The bride and groom should check with the ceremony official that photography is allowed during the ceremony. In most cases it is fine to photograph the arrival and departure of the couple and the signing of the register.

✳ An usher should be assigned the task of keeping a parking space free at the church/venue for the photographer.

✳ The photographer should be provided with a list of the wedding party, family and close friends, and a copy of the table plan. The best man or chief usher should point out who the key players are.

✳ Decide in advance what group shots are required. The best man or chief usher should be given a list of the groups to be photographed so that he can call them together when required.

✳ If there are divorced parents, work out the positioning for the formal shots in advance and inform the photographer of the situation.

✳ Check whether there will be restrictions on reproducing any photographs that include famous guests.

Essential Photographs

Most couples will want to ensure that they have shots of the key moments of the day. Requirements should be discussed with the photographer in advance.

KEY MOMENTS

❋ Getting ready: informal family portraits and shots of the bride, her mother, bridesmaids and pages getting ready; still-life shots of the bride's dress, shoes, jewellery and accessories. It is a good idea to arrange for the photographer to arrive one to two hours before the bride's departure. Black and white is recommended for at least some of these shots.

❋ The ceremony: the groom's party arriving, guests arriving, the groom and best man waiting for the bride, the bride getting out of the car, the service and vows (if photography is allowed), the signing of the register, the bride and groom walking out, and guests milling around after the ceremony is over.

❋ The reception: any formal posed shots should be taken as soon as the bride and groom arrive; the photographer should then take a series of unposed shots of the wedding party and all guests. Still-life photos of the food, canapés, laid tables and behind-the-scenes shots of the caterers will record another dimension of the day.

❋ The speeches and cutting of the cake: this provides an opportunity to capture natural shots of the guests listening and reacting, as well as individual pictures of the wedding party.

❋ The first dance: another chance to capture the bride and groom. Many photographers leave after this point, unless it has been agreed that they will stay later.

❋ Going away: the bride throwing her bouquet and the couple leaving.

SUGGESTED FORMAL PHOTOGRAPHS

These will change according to the family situation.

❋ The bride

❋ The groom

❋ The bride and groom

❋ The bride, groom and her parents

❋ The bride, groom and his parents

❋ The bride, groom and both sets of parents

❋ The bride, chief bridesmaid, bridesmaids and pages

❋ The groom, best man and ushers

❋ The bride, best man and ushers

❋ The groom, chief bridesmaid, bridesmaids and pages

❋ The bride, groom, best man, chief bridesmaid, bridesmaids and pages

❋ The bride, groom and the wedding party

❋ The bride, groom and the bride's grandparents

❋ The bride, groom and the groom's grandparents

❋ The bride, groom and the bride's family (grandparents, uncles, cousins…)

❋ The bride, groom and the groom's family (grandparents, uncles, cousins…)

❋ The bride, groom and friends

On Film

A video captures the essence of the day, along with moments the bride and groom may otherwise miss. Often, however, a cameraman will cost nearly as much as a good photographer. The decision to hire a professional is usually guided by the budget. Some couples will decide to cut costs and simply rely on a good friend instead — many people are now reasonably adept at operating video cameras.

Like the photographer, the person behind the camera will need to be fully briefed on who the key players are, and what the bride and groom expect to be recorded.

PROFESSIONAL

The couple should ask to see an example of previous work and check what the fee includes. There will be different post-production and editing options, the facility to set the film to music (chosen by the couple) and a decision on how many copies of the DVD are to be made. Everything should be built into the final quote.

It is a good idea to have a short synopsis at the start so that the video can be briefly shown to friends; the full-length version may be several hours of footage. A good editor should cut it down to no more than two hours.

NON-PROFESSIONAL

If a wedding guest offers to make a video of the day, the bride and groom will have to accept that the final result will be very different from a professional's film. They may feel that an amateur's attempt, while lacking the finesse of a professional's, is better than no film at all.

The individual must be familiar with the equipment and have practised with it before the big day. It is best to shoot too much than too little; the video can always be cut afterwards. A tripod is essential for the ceremony (if allowed) and the speeches. A spare battery and the camera instruction book are useful in case of emergency.

Transport

There is a wide-ranging choice of transport available for wedding days. No matter how tempting the options – be it a horse and carriage or a London taxi cab – it is imperative to decide on a vehicle that reflects the style of the wedding.

PRACTICALITIES

Practicalities are paramount. A large-skirted wedding dress is not easy to fold into a low-slung sports car; be aware, when choosing open-topped vehicles, that the wind will play havoc with hair, veils and tiaras.

Darker coloured cars look better in photographs as they provide a contrast to the wedding dress. Ribbons should complement and coordinate with the car, rather than dominate it.

HOW MANY?

Normally, two vehicles are required: one for the mother of the bride and the bridesmaids to get to the ceremony, and a second for the father of the bride and the bride. The bride and groom travel from the ceremony to the reception in one car, and the bridesmaids in another. If the budget is restricted, then one car for the bride and her father, and subsequently for the bride and groom, is perfectly acceptable. Alternatively, if the ceremony venue is nearby, one car can be hired to do two trips.

It is essential that the wedding party have cars allocated to them to get to the reception promptly, if needed. Post-ceremony cars are not always essential: if the reception venue is nearby, it is fine for the wedding party to proceed on foot.

TRANSPORT FOR GUESTS

If the location of the wedding is inaccessible, or if parking is limited, transport for the wedding guests may be required. This is usually a coach or bus, or several large taxis. Transport is a budgetary consideration that should not be overlooked; it may be a necessary expense.

The guests can be collected from a specific and easy location – such as a hotel or station – and taken to the ceremony, reception and then back again at the end of the day or evening. Even if parking is available, it is worth considering providing transport for guests: it will allay any anxieties about drinking and driving and ensure that the party goes with a swing.

Alternatively, guests can be supplied with local taxi firm numbers (this may not be efficient in very rural areas where services are limited).

SIGNS AND DIRECTIONS

Make sure signs are clear enough to guide guests travelling by car and any hired transport to the venue;

even a local coach-driver can easily go astray. It is a good idea to delegate to ushers the task of putting up laminated signs at agreed locations, if confusion is likely.

The entrance to the venue must be made obvious. There must be enough room for coaches to turn around. Gate widths must be checked for large vehicles and if coaches are being used, be aware of the hazard of low hanging trees and branches.

GOING AWAY

The going-away vehicle for the bride and groom is usually a taxi. More unusual methods are fun and can be romantic – helicopter, speed boat, open-topped sports car – but the location of the reception and the budget will dictate which choices are available.

Most couples simply decide on a car, be it a classic car or taxi. Traditionally, the going-away vehicle is adorned with tin cans and decorations, such as balloons and streamers, by the best man and ushers. The urge to decorate the car should be resisted if it is a hired vehicle.

Children

The presence of children is often contentious. Some couples welcome children with open arms and see them as a vital part of the day. Other couples favour an adults-only wedding and reception. Either way, a clear decision must be made and adhered to. If children are invited, their names are written on the invitation.

CHILD FRIENDLY

Every effort should be made to make children feel welcome and relaxed. Special provisions, such as a crèche or nanny at the reception, can be considered. A child-friendly menu might be necessary, and children's food may be served earlier than adults'. It may be advisable to seat all the children together with a childminder to keep them occupied, although very small children will probably want to sit with their parents. It is a good idea to provide some form of entertainment or, if the budget allows and there are lots of children, create a separate child-zone with an entertainer and films or cartoons.

ADULTS ONLY

Where children are not invited, this must be clearly stated on the practical information supplied with the invitation. Telling guests can be awkward, so diplomacy must be employed and reasons given, such as limited space. It must be a blanket rule with a specific age cut-off (for example no under-eights); no exceptions should be made, even for close friends.

CHILDREN FROM PREVIOUS RELATIONSHIPS

It is understandable that the bride and groom will want children from previous relationships to be involved in the celebration of their new marriage. Children are often happy to play a special role, such as being a bridesmaid, pageboy or even best man, but they should always be consulted in case they wish to stay in the background. The couple must discuss these issues at an early stage; pressurising children into situations they find uncomfortable might create resentment and uneasiness.

CEREMONIES

Preliminaries

Marriages can take place in England and Wales at a register office, in a building approved for civil marriage (e.g. a stately home or hotel), in a Church of England or Church in Wales parish church, or in any religious building that is registered for the solemnisation of marriage.

The Church of Scotland permits marriages to take place anywhere so long as the minister agrees, the location has a proper address and the couple give notice in the venue's district. In Scotland it is the celebrant, rather than the location, that is licensed. Specific information should be sought for other jurisdictions, as there will be local variations.

This guide supplies information on England and Wales, adding some information for other countries, where relevant. The rules and regulations of marriage must be complied with. Here are some important points:

※ The ceremony must take place in the presence of a superintendent registrar or an authorised person (e.g. vicar or priest) and be witnessed by at least two competent people, who also sign the marriage register.

※ The minimum legal age is 16, but under-18s must obtain written consent from their legal guardians. In Scotland, marriage at 16 doesn't require parental consent; different rules apply in Jersey and Guernsey.

※ A couple may not marry if either of them is currently married to someone else.

※ The bride and groom must not be directly related, either as blood or adoptive relatives. Step-parents and children can marry if both parties are over 21 and the younger partner has not lived in the house with, or been raised by, the elder partner. In such cases, special ecclesiastical licenses are required for church weddings.

※ The marriage must take place between 8 a.m. and 6 p.m. This doesn't apply to Jewish or Muslim weddings.

※ The civil preliminaries must be complied with for any marriage or registration of civil partnership (registration of a same sex couple) taking place in a register office or approved venue, and for all religious marriages other than the Church of England or Church in Wales.

HOW MUCH DOES IT COST TO GET MARRIED?
In 2007, the rates are as follows:

※ Giving notice in advance of a ceremony either at a register office, approved premises or in a religious building other than in the Church of England or Church in Wales: £30.00 per person.

※ Register office ceremony/registration of civil partnership: £40.00.

※ Ceremony on approved premises – the cost for attendance by the superintendent registrar and registrar is set by the local authority in question. The owners of the building may also charge for the use of the premises.

※ Church of England or Church in Wales ceremony – the legal fees for a church marriage cover the publication of the banns, the marriage service and a certificate of marriage. These fees are fixed centrally across all parish churches, and will be in the region of £240. They do not include any extras, such as an organist, bell-ringers or a choir, or fees for video recording.

※ Religious ceremony at a building other than Church of England or Church in Wales – £47.00 for the registrar. Further fees may be charged by the trustees of the building and by the person who performs the ceremony.

※ Marriage certificate: £3.50.

Forms are then sent to the couple, who must sign and return them enclosing all relevant documentation, such as birth certificates, death certificates or divorce decree absolutes for the widowed/divorced, and identification, including proof of nationality.

English and Welsh civil marriage laws apply equally to both UK and overseas citizens, but for the latter some additional documentation will need to be supplied.

After giving notice, 15 clear days must then pass before the marriage can take place. For example, if notice is given on 11 June, the ceremony can take place on or after 27 June.

It is best to give four to six weeks' notice if possible and, if either party has been married previously, six weeks is the compulsory notice period.

The notice of marriage is valid for 12 months, but it is sometimes possible to make an advance booking to extend this period with the relevant superintendent registrar of the district in which the wedding is going to take place.

Both the bride and groom must have lived in a registration district in England, Wales or Scotland for at least seven days prior to giving notice at the register office.

As long as one person is resident in England and Wales, the other person may also give notice of marriage in Scotland.

Provided the person they intend to marry is resident in England and Wales, officers, seamen or marines on board one of Her Majesty's ships at sea can give notice to the captain or other officer commanding the ship.

CIVIL PRELIMINARIES

'Giving notice' is the term used to describe the commencement of civil marriage proceedings. The bride and groom must give notice, in person, to the superintendent registrar in the district in which they live (this is a legal requirement). If they live in different registration districts, they must give notice separately in each district, or visit their local register office together.

They must also give notice, in person, to the superintendent registrar in the district in which the marriage is due to take place. This is a practical requirement ensuring that the superintendent registrar (to conduct the service) and a registrar of marriages (to record the details in the marriage register and issue the marriage certificate) will be free to attend the chosen venue on the wedding day.

The Church of England

✤

All British citizens can marry in the Church of England or Church in Wales parish church where they are resident, or where one of the couple is on the church's electoral roll (this is different from the local register of electors). The bride and groom need not necessarily be regular churchgoers or be baptised.

The marriage ceremony traditionally takes place in the bride's parish church. If the chosen church is not in the local parish of either of the bride or groom, then it must be the usual place of worship for one of them and they must be listed on the church's electoral roll.

To qualify for enrolment, at least one partner must have regularly attended that church for a minimum period of six months, and the person must be a baptised member of the Church of England. If there is a special connection with a church which is not their parish church, it may be possible to apply for an Archbishop's Special Licence.

PREPARATIONS

The couple should contact the parish priest at an early stage when looking to book the church. The priest will usually want to meet them to discuss arrangements and possible dates and times, and may even offer marriage preparation sessions. It is usual to run through the intended hymns, readings and any other requests – such as saying vows without his or her prompting – with the priest. The wedding may take place on a Sunday, but this is rare. It is common practice for ministers to refuse to conduct marriages during Lent and often during Advent.

SECOND MARRIAGES

If either the bride or groom is divorced, they may meet resistance if they wish to re-marry in a church. Anglican priests are entitled to refuse to marry divorcees, although some priests are happy to do so. If a priest can't be persuaded, there is no method of appeal. A civil ceremony followed by a blessing in church is one option.

THE BANNS

The civil preliminaries do not need to be followed for an Anglican wedding. The usual means of announcing an intended marriage is the publication of the banns. These are read in the parish church where the wedding will take place and in the parish churches of both the bride and groom (if these are different) on three consecutive Sundays within three months prior to the marriage. The couple are usually present for at least one announcement.

The other forms are common licence (where only a day's notice is needed, often used where there is an imminent and unavoidable departure overseas), special licence (i.e. for a church which is not the couple's parish church, but holds special meaning for them), and by authority of the Superintendent Registrar's office (where relatives-in-law wish to marry). The priest will advise the couple if and when any of these more rare formalities are needed.

THE CEREMONY

The bride's family and friends will sit on the left hand side of the church, facing the alter, and the groom's on the right. Parents sit on the front row, grandparents and siblings in the next and close family behind. Seating should be reserved for bridesmaids (at the front) and ushers.

The ushers ask guests whether they are a friend/relative of the bride or groom. If they're friends of both, they should be given the best available spot.

If one family has more guests than the other, guests can be seated from front to back, regardless of sides, to balance things out. The ushers should inform guests that this is the case as they enter the church, and guests can then choose where to sit.

A church service lasts around 45 minutes and follows a set formula. The music, hymns and readings are chosen by the couple. The service is in either modern (Common Worship) or traditional wording (the Book of Common Prayer); this is the priest's decision and the couple do not normally have a choice.

SAMPLE RUNNING ORDER

❋ Music: this is played, usually on the organ, while the congregation arrive and settle into their seats. The groom and best man take their place in the front pew, on the right hand side facing the altar.

❋ Entrance of the bride: once the bride is in position, the processional music begins. She is accompanied down the aisle by her father, or the person appointed to give her away, who stands on the bride's left.

❋ The Greeting: the priest welcomes the congregation and the couple, briefly describing the purpose and format of the service.

❋ Hymn

❋ Readings: usually given by family members or close friends – preferably by those with clear voices and a confident delivery.

❋ The Address: this may, with the priest's consent, be given by a family member or friend (who will often be a member of the clergy).

❋ Hymn

❋ The Marriage: the Vows (usually spoken quietly by the priest and recited loudly by the bride and groom so that the congregation can hear), the Giving of Rings, the Proclamation (where the priest announces the union of the bride and groom before God). Finally, the couple will kneel at the High Altar for the Blessing of the Marriage.

❋ Signing of the Register: the civil (legal) element of the wedding. The register must be signed by both bride and groom, the minister and then two to four witnesses (often chief bridesmaid, best man, and perhaps family members). The bride signs her maiden name, perhaps for the last time.

During the Signing of the Register, a choral or solo item may be performed.

❋ The prayers

❋ Hymn

❋ Recessional: appropriate music will be played as the bride and groom leave the church. The bridal party follows – father of the bride accompanies mother of the groom, father of the groom accompanies mother of the bride, and the best man walks with the chief bridesmaid.

The Church of England: Details

HOW LATE IS FASHIONABLY LATE?

It is traditionally the bride's prerogative to arrive 'fashionably late'. Regarded with almost superstitious fervour by some and as pointless by others, consideration should be given to the groom. The longer she leaves it, the longer he is left at the front of the church, which can become embarrassing. Even if the bride's car pulls up on time, she will probably still be late, as it can take a good five minutes to get out of the car, meet the priest and compose herself.

The belief that a little anticipation might make the bride's entrance all the more thrilling when she does at last begin processing down the aisle can introduce unnecessary tension. The bride should allow a few minutes to regain her composure and arrange the dress, veil, bouquet and so on.

THE VOWS: TO LOVE, HONOUR AND 'OBEY'

The Church of England is unique in including this word in its vows – while the bride promises to 'obey', the groom vows to 'worship' his wife. The couple are perfectly free to omit these words; an alternative that many couples choose is 'to love and to honour'.

THE ORDER OF SERVICE

There is no standard format for the order of service sheet; the couple are free to choose how much detail they wish to include. There are, however, some customary guidelines.

On the front cover are the Christian names or initials of the bride and groom, the name of the church and the date, and perhaps time, of the service. Inside, the order of service will usually include titles of music, hymns and readings and often the composer or author. It may be advisable to include the full text of hymns; this dispenses with the need for hymn books, which have to be located, opened and shared.

If the choir is using a hymn book instead of the service sheet, ensure that the words are the same. This can be checked in advance by borrowing a hymn book from the church and using it to compile the order of service. Don't rely on printers, who could have a different book from the one used by the church.

The order of service lists the various stages of the service. A personal touch could be added by including a poem or saying on either the inside front cover or inside back cover. This isn't read out; it is just something for the congregation to muse upon.

It is customary to acknowledge the minister and/or registrar by name, and to credit the organist, choir or group of musicians who perform during the ceremony. Some couples also like to list the key members of the wedding party such as the best man, ushers, chief bridesmaid, bridesmaids and pages. Readers' names should accompany the text/title of their reading.

Most couples opt for a simple cream or white folded card, matching the invitation in style and size. Printing costs will vary according to size and the level of detail included. It is possible to add crests, illustrations or monograms but, for optimum cohesion, the order of service should ideally match the invitations. Ribbons or tassels are a pretty touch, but may detract from the elegance of the design.

If the task of compiling the order of service is left to a company specialising in producing wedding stationery, proofs should be checked very carefully to ensure that the hymns and readings are the correct version and that there are no mistakes. Checking for grammatical errors, punctuation and spelling is vital. Look in particular at names and dates, as this is where common errors occur. Once edited and returned, the order of service can be printed and delivered well ahead of the day.

MUSIC

Music can play a very important role in establishing the atmosphere in church. Reflect on past weddings and think about what worked and what was not so successful, and build on those impressions. A meeting with the church's organist can be a good way to begin selecting the music for the service, particularly if the bride and groom are not quite sure what they want.

Music is an area where it is worth spending money: invest in the church's organist and choir and the congregation are more likely to join in with the hymns. Any deficiencies in the congregation's singing will also be well concealed.

Some companies are dedicated to providing a complete wedding music package, from organists and trumpeters for the ceremony to DJs and jazz bands for the evening's events. Professional organists, choirs and soloists can be hired on an individual basis – a quick search on the internet or asking friends for suggestions will yield countless results. A cautionary note: when professional musicians are used, they will expect an enhanced fee – often double the original – if the service is being videoed.

When choosing hymns it is important to consider how well known they are, and how easy they are to sing but, equally, the best-known hymns or songs may not be appropriate for this particular occasion. A well loved sporting anthem or school song (for example 'Jerusalem', or 'Swing Low Sweet Chariot') might not have quite the same rousing effect on one's wedding day.

Three hymns is the norm – at the beginning, in the middle and at the end of the service. This gives the proceedings structure, and the congregation will feel included by taking an active role at these key points. If communion is taken during the service, a fourth hymn may be sung afterwards.

Civil Ceremonies

A civil ceremony has no religious aspects. Couples can marry at a register office or approved venue in England, Wales or Scotland. There is no requirement that either or both partners live in the venue's district.

PREPARATIONS

The superintendent registrar of the district where the wedding will take place should be contacted, and the civil preliminaries followed. Ceremonies are permitted on any day of the week between 8 a.m. and 6 p.m., but most register offices are open Monday to Friday 10 a.m.– 4 p.m. and on Saturdays 10 a.m.–1 p.m. At least two other people over the age of 18 (16 in Scotland) must be present to act as witnesses and sign the marriage register.

THE CEREMONY: REGISTER OFFICE

A register office ceremony is relatively short – normally approximately 20 minutes in duration. The ceremony will usually follow a traditional format, interspersed with music and readings, which must be agreed on in advance with the registrar.

The groom and best man may choose to await the arrival of the bride at the front. Guests will be then be asked to stand for the entrance of the bride, who will be escorted by her father or other male relative. Alternatively, the couple will process to the front together. The registrar announces the intention of the couple to be married and requests any person present who knows of any impediment to declare it.

All civil marriages must then incorporate a statutory declaration and contracting statements, which are recited by both bride and groom. There are various forms of wording that can be used: the couple should discuss their choice of words with the superintendent registrar if they do not want to use the traditional statements. Additionally, specially written vows or statements might be used, but this is at the discretion of the registrar.

Once the declaratory words have been spoken, the bride, groom, registrar and witnesses sign the register. The registrar announces that the couple are married, and will usually lead the wedding party from the venue, often accompanied by music.

THE CEREMONY: APPROVED VENUE

An approved venue is one that has been licensed for civil marriage ceremonies – such as a stately home or hotel. The legal requirements are the same as for register office weddings. Notice is given at the couple's local registries but, apart from organising for the local registrar to attend the ceremony, there is no requirement to give formal notice to the superintendent registrar of the registration district. Once the superintendent registrar has been booked, the venue can be confirmed. Licensed venues have the benefit of more flexible hours than register offices, but the marriage must still take place within the legal times.

The ceremony can be more relaxed and leisurely than in a register office, and some formalities can be dispensed with. The attending registrar must approve all choices and, so long as he or she is amenable, non religious music and readings can be used.

It may also be possible for a couple to write their own vows and promises; these are used in addition to the statutory declaratory and contracting words that are legally required to be said by the bride and groom.

A HUMANIST CEREMONY

A humanist wedding is a non-denominational celebration of a couple's love, often held in a garden or marquee. The bride and groom can write every word of the ceremony. It is not a legally binding ceremony; a separate register office marriage will have to take place or, if it is taking place at a venue that is licensed for weddings, a registrar can perform the legal elements during the ceremony.

ORDER OF THE DAY

Rather like the order of service for church weddings, it is a good idea to provide guests with an order of ceremony, in which the significant points of the proceedings are listed. Alternatively, create an order of the day, guiding guests through the entire proceedings.

MUSIC

A civil ceremony must not contain religious references, so hymns are not permitted. Popular music, folk songs, ballet, classical music or opera are usually acceptable, but should be carefully checked for religious connotations.

There is likely to be music as the guests are seated, for the entrance of the bride, during the signing of the register and as the couple exit.

Do remember that whatever music is chosen must first be agreed to by the superintendent registrar.

A CHURCH BLESSING?

A service of prayer and dedication may follow a civil ceremony where the couple wish to add a religious element to their marriage – not necessarily on the same day, but this is often the case.

Where it has been difficult to book a church wedding due to circumstances such as a previous divorce, this provides a satisfactory compromise for both the church and the couple as most ministers will agree to preside over a service of blessing.

During the service, the minister will usually give a brief address and prayers are said to bless the marriage. The questions of what to wear, the number of guests, flowers and music should be discussed with the priest. There are no legal requirements or set fees.

CIVIL PARTNERSHIPS

The registration of civil partnerships became legal in December 2005. They are not 'marriages' in the legal sense of the word, but legal recognition of gay and lesbian relationships.

A civil partnership gives partners the same legal rights as a heterosexual married couple in respect of pension rights, house ownership, inheritance issues and making next-of-kin decisions in hospital.

The civil preliminaries must be complied with once the couple has chosen where they'd like the ceremony to be held. It can take place in any licensed venue in the UK, be it a register office, castle or hotel.

The law does not provide for a specific ceremony. The partners sign a document before the registrar and two witnesses, and music, readings and vows can be included. All choices will need to be approved by the registrar, and nothing may be of a religious nature.

Roman Catholic

The civil preliminaries must be completed; the couple must register their intention to marry and obtain the marriage licence from the superintendent registrar. It is usual for them to marry at their local church, but permission may be obtained from the Roman Catholic authorities to be married in another church. If the church is in a different registration district from where the couple live, they must prove to the superintendent registrar that it is their normal place of worship, or they must give notice in the church's registration district after having met the necessary civil residence requirement.

PREPARATIONS

The first step is to consult the priest or minister in the parish(es) where the bride and groom reside. This is required by the Church and the State in adherence with the need to ascertain 'freedom to marry'. If the bride and groom are Catholic, there are forms to complete to declare that both are legally and spiritually able to marry, that they freely intend to marry and that they agree with the Church's view of marriage – namely that it is one of the seven Sacraments and represents a lifelong commitment to God. The publication of banns will then proceed, but they are not a legal requirement. If one party is not Catholic, a dispensation must be obtained from the priest or bishop to permit the marriage.

It is advisable to give the priest six months' notice. Several meetings will be held to discuss the arrangements for the wedding. The priest will advise on the service, including selecting the hymns, readings and psalms.

SECOND MARRIAGES

Marriage of divorcees is unheard of in the Catholic Church. Divorces by non-Catholics are not recognised, so these individuals are considered to be married. Thus remarriage of a non-Catholic to a Catholic will not be permitted; a limited number of priests may offer a blessing if both parties are regular churchgoers.

THE CEREMONY

- The Rite of Marriage During Mass is usually adopted when both partners are Catholic. Holy Communion is offered to the bride, groom and all Catholic members of the congregation. The vows form part of the Mass and are inserted into the liturgy after scripture readings.

- The Rite of Marriage Outside Mass is more common when one party is a non-Catholic or when the couple wish to have a shorter ceremony.

Upon entering the church, Catholic guests will make the sign of the cross and perhaps genuflect (bend the knee) as a mark of respect. Guests of other denominations and faiths aren't expected to follow suit.

The bride, on the arm of her father (or other appointed male), proceeds down the aisle to the groom and priest. Alternatively, the guests assemble in the church porch to greet the couple as they arrive. The bride and groom then walk with the priest down the aisle towards the altar, followed by the guests.

The order and content of the service depends on which Rite of Marriage the couple have chosen. The bride and groom will exchange vows and then the ring(s) will be blessed by the priest before being exchanged. The priest says a prayer and the couple are invited to seal their union with a kiss, unless they have chosen to have a Mass, in which case they will kiss once Mass has been said. After the final blessing, the bride, groom and wedding party move to the sacristy to make the civil declaration and sign the register. A hymn of thanksgiving may be sung during the signing of the register. Finally, the newly married couple process out of the church.

Music and order of service sheet: the same considerations as the Church of England apply.

Other Faiths and Denominations

In terms of religion, the UK is a truly eclectic society. There is often a great deal of variation within individual faiths, depending on the level of conformity of the families involved. Specific advice should, of course, be sought for individual faiths and denominations, and guests should do their research before attending a ceremony whose format and traditions will be unfamiliar.

CHURCH OF SCOTLAND WEDDING

The civil preliminaries must be completed; the registrar need not be present at the service if intent to marry has been presented to the registrar at least 15 days before the wedding. There are no residency requirements.

NONCONFORMIST CHURCH WEDDING

Marriages in Protestant churches, other than the Church of England, follow similar procedures to marriages in the Roman Catholic Church. The civil preliminaries must be observed. If the church is in a different registration district from where the couple live, they need to prove to the superintendent registrar that the church is their place of worship. Otherwise, notice is given in the church's registration district and the residency requirement met. If there is no church of the desired denomination in the registration district in which the couple live, they can marry in the nearest registration district that has one. A superintendent registrar attends the ceremony if the minister is not authorised to register marriages. If the chosen church is not registered for the solemnisation of marriage, a civil ceremony takes place beforehand.

QUAKER MARRIAGE

An application is made to the registering officer at the Society of Friends' monthly meeting where the marriage ceremony is to take place. If only one partner is a member of the Society, the other is asked to state their sympathies with the nature of the marriage and they must provide letters of recommendation from two other members. The registering officer issues a form that is taken to the superintendent registrar when notice is given – the civil preliminaries must be complied with. If the building in which the couple wish to marry is in a different registration district to the area where they live, the procedures in the 'Nonconformist' section apply.

MUSLIM MARRIAGE

The civil preliminaries must be completed, and the only notice period required is that dictated by British civil law; there is no additional notice required, and the marriage can take place at any time of day.

The Islamic religion recommends that a couple should be well acquainted before marriage is considered, but they aren't permitted to be alone in a closed room or go out together unchaperoned. Marriages may be arranged by the parents, but the couple must agree to the union.

To validate the wedding, a *Mahr* (the bride's wedding gift) is offered by the husband. Regarded as a token of commitment, this may be cash, property, other material goods or a non-material offering such as a promise to teach the bride to read the holy texts. It can be paid immediately or at a later date; a deferred *Mahr* remains due after death or following the couple's divorce.

It is forbidden for Muslims to marry on the two days of Eid, occurring after the feast of Ramadan, the Day of the Pilgrimage or the Day of Ashura, which falls on the ninth or tenth day of the Islamic first month, Muharran. Any other date, at any time of day, is permitted.

Weddings are usually well attended, although the basic requirement is only that two male witnesses are present. The *Al Nikah* (ceremony) typically lasts about an hour and a half and begins with an address given by the officiator, who can be any worthy Muslim. The sermon invites the bride and groom and their guests to lead a life of piety, kindness, love and social responsibility.

Beginning with the praise of Allah, His help and guidance is sought. This is followed by the Muslim confession of faith: 'There is none worthy of worship except Allah, and Muhammad is His servant and messenger'. Then three Qur'anic verses (Qur'an 4:1, 3:102, 33:70–71) and the *Hadith* (a prophetic saying) form the main text of the marriage. The ceremony is concluded by the officiator, with prayers for the newly-weds, their families and the community in general. The *Walima* – celebration banquet – is hosted by the groom.

HINDU MARRIAGE

Hindu wedding ceremonies aren't recognised by British law and therefore must be accompanied by a civil marriage in a register office (civil preliminaries apply). Traditional Hindu weddings can last several days; they usually take place outside under a *Mandap* (canopy). Only the rituals most significant to the individuals and their families are included in modern weddings, which last about an hour.

Astrological charts are consulted to select the wedding date; weddings are not permitted on Amas (one day each month), during Shraaddh (a two-week period during September) and 15 days before the festival of Holi. The Hindu calendar is consulted to assess when these key dates fall each year. The couple usually meet the male Brahmin (priest) who advises them on the ceremony.

The venue is the choice of the bride's family and tends to be a town hall or hotel. Blessings in the temple follow the service. A sacred fire, *Agni*, is placed in a central position. Shoes must not be worn under the *Mandap*.

The multitude of rituals and traditions mean that the format cannot be predicted, but some popular modern day practices can often be observed. The *Sangeet Sandhya* is an evening of musical entertainment when the groom's family entertain the bride and groom. Henna is applied

to the bride's hands and feet (and to the groom's if he wishes), this is known as *Mehendi Lagwana*. On the right hand, a round spot is left open for *Hathlewa*, which occurs later. The groom leaves for the wedding venue upon a decorated horse, as part of a very grand and very colourful procession known as *Barat Nikasi*. The *Panditji* puts a coin on the groom's right hand and ties his hand to the bride's hand. This ritual is called *Hathlewa*.

The actual marriage ceremony is called the *Havan*. The priest ties the end of the groom's kurta or dhoti to the end of the bride's sari, symbolising sacred wedlock. The bride and groom circle the holy fire seven times, making seven promises to be fulfilled in married life. After this they are considered married. During *Kanya Daan*, the father of the bride pours sacred water, symbolising the giving away of the bride, and demands of the groom a promise to make the new bride happy.

Other Faiths and Denominations

SIKH MARRIAGE

A Sikh wedding, or *Anand Karaj*, is a very family-oriented event with a festive atmosphere. Marriages are usually arranged by the families, in agreement with the bride and groom. Increasingly the couple choose each other and then seek the approval of their families.

The Official Sikh Code of Conduct expressly forbids any sort of dowry arrangement, and any two Sikhs may be joined in matrimony regardless of caste, race or lineage. The ceremony can be performed in any *Gurdwara* (temple), or in a home where the Sikh Holy Scripture has been respectfully installed, but may not be performed in a hotel or banqueting hall. *Anand Karaj* is not restricted to certain dates or times, but is usually conducted in the mornings and takes several hours at most.

The *Kurmai* is the traditional Sikh engagement ceremony, sometimes performed a week before the wedding. If it takes place in the *Gurdwara* it will involve prayer, hymns and a meal, but if it is held at the groom's home the bride's family visit for a short time and present the groom with Indian sweets. In return the groom's family present the bride with an Indian suit and some sweets.

Guests should never wear white (it is deemed unlucky), but instead should wear deep, vibrant colours such as reds and purples; men and women must wear a head covering. Shoes are removed at the venue's entrance.

Variations in the *Anand Karaj* ceremony tend to be minimal. In the West, weddings are usually a one- or two-day affair; the wedding either occurs in the morning followed by a dinner and dance, or the religious ceremony and banquet take place on consecutive days.

On the day, the bride's family wait in the venue and the groom arrives with his family in procession, traditionally on horseback. There may be a light meal before the ceremony, and garlands are exchanged. Male and female guests are normally seated separately, though non-Sikh men and women may be seated together.

The religious ceremony is conducted by the *Pathi* (any respected Sikh man or woman) and begins after the officiant has ascertained that both bride and groom are Sikh and has asked for public consent to the union. Every time the bride or groom stand or sit during the ceremony, they bow down to the Sikh Holy Scripture to show respect, with their foreheads touching the ground. The father of the bride makes a symbolic gesture that his daughter is leaving his care for that of her husband by placing one end of a sash worn by the groom in his daughter's hand.

JEWISH MARRIAGE

The civil preliminaries apply, and special arrangements are made if the couple wish to marry in a venue outside the registration district in which they live. Rabbinical law requires that a Jewish ceremony is performed under a *Chuppah* (a wedding canopy). A synagogue is the usual venue; less traditional weddings take place at secular locations such as hotels, but always under the *Chuppah*.

The format of a wedding depends upon the branch of Judaism to which the bride and/or groom belong. Sundays and Tuesdays are the most popular days to marry; the Sabbath, Holy Days and fasting periods are not permitted.

It is customary for the bride and groom not to see each other for at least a day before the wedding. The ancient ritual of the bride's immersion in a *mikvah* (ritual pool) several days prior to the wedding is still widely practised. The bride and groom fast on the day, from first light until the ceremony, in repentance for past sins. Guests at Orthodox synagogue weddings should dress modestly. Reform and Liberal ceremonies are more relaxed, but shoulders should be covered and, traditionally, married women's heads should be covered. Male guests cover their heads with a *Yarmulke* (skullcap).

The Orthodox ceremony follows a fixed liturgy, which all variations of Jewish weddings stem from, and will last about 45 minutes. The *Minyan*, a group of at least ten adult Jewish males, must be present. A Jewish wedding often includes combinations of, and variations on, rituals.

Men and women are often seated separately. The groom arrives with his father, who escorts him to stand under the *Chuppah* (under which no jewellery may be worn). The groom is formally requested to approve of the two chosen witnesses and to accept the terms of the *Ketubah* (marriage contract). The raising of a pen or handkerchief, and the signing the *Ketubah* by the witnesses, indicates this acceptance. The act is known as making a *Kinyan*.

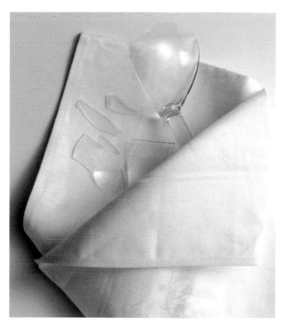

Upon entering the synagogue, the bride is taken to the *Bedekken* room, the groom confirms her identity and the couple are blessed by the rabbi. The service continues in the main synagogue into which the bride is traditionally escorted by the two mothers; at some weddings she will walk around the groom seven times under the canopy. This is followed by the Chant of Welcome and the rabbi's recital of the betrothal blessings over a cup of wine, from which the bride and groom drink.

The groom performs the marriage by putting a ring on the forefinger of the bride's right hand in the presence of two religiously-qualified witnesses and the rabbi. The ring is later transferred onto the ring finger of the left hand. The rabbi recites the Seven Marriage Benedictions over a second cup of wine from which the couple drink, before the groom crushes a glass object (wrapped in a napkin) with his foot. Finally, the civil registers are signed, and the couple spend a few moments in a private room. The congregation wait for the wedding party to leave the synagogue before making their exit.

A meal after the ceremony is customary, and at least a *Minyan* should be present. Celebrations include circle dancing, where the bride and groom are lifted above the heads of the guests. If either is the last child in their family to marry, a dance is performed for the parents to celebrate the successful marriage of all of their children.

MIXED FAITH WEDDINGS

Where the bride and groom are of different faiths, they will usually need to decide which is to be the most dominant influence in the marriage service, and seek the permission of their religious celebrant to include concessions to the other faith within the ceremony. This is most common when a Catholic marries in the Church of England tradition, when the priest may be happy to invite an officiant from the other denomination to give an address or bless the couple.

THE
WEDDING
TEAM

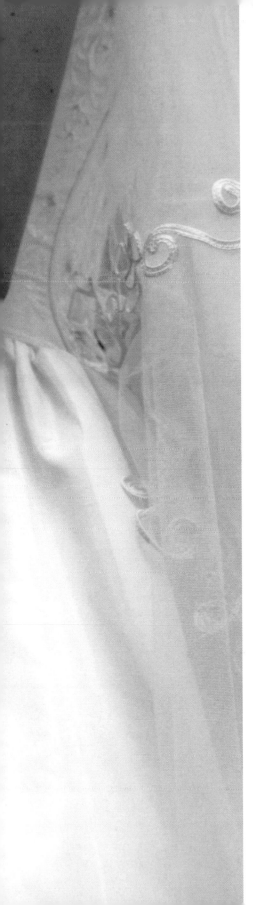

The Bride and Groom

Traditionally it was the bride and her mother who took responsibility for organising the wedding. It is now increasingly likely that the bride and groom will make the majority of the decisions.

While parents should be consulted, especially if they are contributing to or financing the wedding, the bride and groom usually make final decisions on key elements of the day, such as the style of reception, food, drink, entertainment, the wedding list and transport.

JOINT RESPONSIBILITIES

⬧ Discussing and deciding upon the choice of ceremony (religious/civil). Choosing music, hymns and readings.

⬧ Deciding how many people will be invited to the ceremony and the reception; confronting any fragile family situations from the very start.

⬧ Exploring and deciding upon the style of the day.

⬧ Looking for suitable venues, and planning how the day will be structured. Food, drink and entertainment choices will follow.

⬧ Thinking about the logistics of the day, such as transport and timings.

⬧ Drawing up a wedding list.

⬧ Discussing and choosing members of the wedding team – the best man, ushers and bridesmaids – and making sure both are happy with the choices.

⬧ Communicating with each other to ensure that both remain fully informed of arrangements.

⬧ Buying each other a wedding ring.

Responsibilities of the Bride

There are certain things that the bride must plan and organise. Depending on how the wedding is being structured, the bride's mother may help her here.

Choosing the bridal party – chief bridesmaid and adult bridesmaids, baby bridesmaids or pageboys – and making her expectations of them known. Deciding on and choosing their outfits and ensuring that they fit properly.

Choosing a wedding dress, jewellery, shoes, veil, headpiece and other accessories.

Booking a hairdresser, manicurist and make-up artist, if required. Deciding whether other members of the bridal party – mother, chief bridesmaid and adult bridesmaids – will need their hair and make-up done.

Advising the chief bridesmaid of any expectations she may have for the hen party, and who she wants to attend.

Booking the cars to take the bridal party to the church: one for the bride and her father (or the person giving her away), and another for the mother of the bride and the bridesmaids or pages. The rest of the transport is arranged by the groom.

Choosing all the flowers for the ceremony venue and the reception. Traditionally, the groom pays for the bouquets and buttonholes; most brides, however, prefer to take charge of this.

Overseeing the writing of thank you letters when the couple return from honeymoon.

Responsibilities of the Groom

The groom must be involved and consulted at every step, but there are a number of responsibilities that are traditionally his alone. The best man is there to help the groom fulfil his duties.

🔲 Overseeing the legalities (e.g. reading of the banns) and practicalities (e.g. payment) of the ceremony.

🔲 Choosing and fully briefing the best man and ushers. Explaining what they are expected to wear.

🔲 Advising the best man of any expectations he may have for the stag night, and who he wants to attend.

🔲 Taking possession of the wedding rings and handing them to the best man on the day.

🔲 Arranging the transport to the ceremony venue for himself and the best man, and from the ceremony venue to the reception for himself and the bride.

🔲 Traditionally, paying for the bouquets and the buttonholes; many brides will handle all the flowers.

🔲 Buying thank you presents for the bridesmaids, pages, best man and ushers. Traditionally, the mothers should also receive a present or bouquet.

🔲 Organising a hotel or equivalent for the wedding night and booking the honeymoon.

🔲 Delivering a speech, and remembering to thank everyone involved.

Choosing the Team

The bride and best man must get on well. She should have confidence that he will successfully perform his duties up to and on the day. Likewise, the groom should have confidence in the chief bridesmaid.

PREPARING THE TEAM

The numbers and composition of the bridal party must be carefully considered. A manageable bridal party could consist of, for example: a chief bridesmaid, two adult bridesmaids and then a pageboy or child bridesmaid; one chief bridesmaid and three children; or just three children. The options are endless, but practicalities should be thought through.

The general rule is to have one usher for every 50 guests although many grooms choose to have more, to involve close friends in the day.

The wedding team is essential in ensuring that the big day runs smoothly. Members should know the couple well and the key players – the best man, bridesmaids and ushers – must be chosen carefully.

The couple need to be practical about the character traits of those they are considering. Are they able to handle responsibility? Can they cope with organisation? Are they easily overwhelmed? Sometimes close friends are unsuitable and more capable individuals must be chosen instead; there will be plenty of less demanding jobs for the others. At this stage, the couple should also decide whether they want children as bridesmaids or pageboys.

TEAM LEADERS

The most important positions to be filled are those of best man and chief bridesmaid. The people chosen need to be reliable, quick thinking and skilled organisers. They must also be able to delegate jobs to the ushers and bridesmaids, as well as solve problems and mediate delicate situations if required.

Ushers and other bridesmaids will have limited duties before the day, but they must understand what is expected of them and be aware of the responsibilities they are taking on right from the start. It must never be assumed that members of the wedding party will know what to do. Time should be allowed to fully brief the team well before the wedding.

If the team don't know each other it is wise to arrange some get-togethers before the wedding, which will ease any unfamiliar awkwardness at the hen and stag parties. Also, the better the wedding team knows each other, and their traits, the better they will work together on the day.

Parents come as part of the package and their role is entirely dependent on how the bride and groom decide to conduct their wedding arrangements. Parents' influence is often directly proportionate to their financial input. It is an added bonus, and will help the day go more smoothly, if the best man and the chief bridesmaid are familiar with the parents of the bride and groom.

The Best Man's Role

One of the greatest compliments a man can pay a friend is to ask him to be best man at his wedding. The best man is taking on a major role and must be willing to commit fully to the task. Forward planning and good organisational skills are key.

High levels of diplomacy, confidence, thoughtfulness and reliability are needed. The best man will be involved during the planning stages, so he must be willing to dedicate a considerable amount of time in the run-up to the actual wedding day.

There is much more to the role than organising an unforgettable stag night and making a funny speech: with the privilege of the position comes a huge amount of responsibility. He must make sure that the day runs as smoothly as possible and that everyone is fulfilling their duties, whilst also being the groom's prop.

BEFORE THE BIG DAY

The groom should ensure that the best man understands his expectations. The bride and groom should make the best man aware of any sensitive family situations, such as divorce or estrangement, well ahead of the day. Some pre-wedding research is recommended: it is helpful if the best man is familiar with, or at least able to recognise, key people on the day (parents, grandparents, very close friends of the family and godparents).

The best man must liaise with the chief bridesmaid to ensure that all tasks and duties are fulfilled in the run-up to the wedding and on the day itself. He should be available for at least a week before the wedding to assist with any last minute dilemmas or problems.

EVENT MANAGEMENT

On the day, the best man must work discreetly and efficiently to ensure that everything is running to plan; he will be the first point of contact if there is a crisis. He is the intermediary between the groom and the ushers and is the groom's voice as far as requests and instructions are concerned.

The best man can also be the master of ceremonies if there is not a separate person in this role. He will announce the bride and groom, the lunch/dinner and introduce the speakers and speeches.

As an alternative, the best man's duties can be split between two individuals. Generally, this involves one person who looks after the logistics of the ceremony and the reception and another who attends the groom on the day. One of them can make the speech, or they could join forces and do it together.

It is, however, more advisable to choose just one best man and then have a supporting chief usher with specific duties to fulfil.

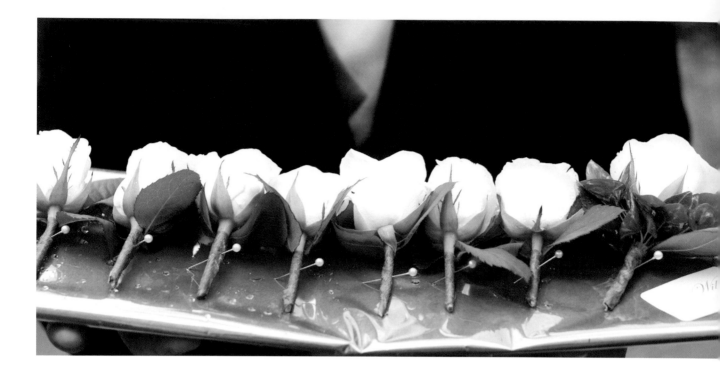

The Best Man's Duties

BEFORE THE DAY

※ Arranging a stag night or weekend at least several weeks in advance of the wedding day.

※ Making sure the ushers have the correct clothes and know what is expected of them on the day.

※ Meeting up with the bride and groom's parents and the bridesmaids before the day.

※ Visiting the ceremony and reception venues. Becoming familiar with their layout and the timetable of events.

※ Attending the rehearsal and introducing people that might not know each other.

WEDDING DUTIES

※ Staying with the groom the night before the wedding.

※ Running through the day with the groom and checking that he has everything he needs (not forgetting the rings).

※ Accompanying the groom to the ceremony venue in good time (at least 45 minutes in advance) and staying with him in the lead-up to the service. Initially he should be outside ready to welcome ushers and guests, and then take up position next to the groom, waiting for the bride's arrival.

※ Making himself known to the ceremony officiate in case there are any problems before or during the service.

Casting an eye over the venue and checking that family and guests are being seated correctly. Looking out for a nod from the chief usher to say the bride has arrived.

Handing over the ring(s) at the critical moment.

Joining the bridal party in the vestry/register, and then accompanying the chief bridesmaid down the aisle.

Ensuring that the bride and groom are ready to have their photographs taken; getting them into the car (or equivalent) that will take them to the reception.

Checking that the bridesmaids, families of the bride and groom and ushers are shown to the correct cars for the journey to the reception.

Having the money ready if any payments (for the church or band) are required on the day.

Circulating and introducing guests at the reception.

Liaising with the chief bridesmaid and ensuring that everything is going to plan. If there are any problems, remaining calm and quietly sorting them out, preferably without the bride and groom knowing.

Delivering his speech. The best man shouldn't drink too much until the speeches are over.

Ensuring that the first night/honeymoon luggage, tickets and passports are in the correct get-away vehicle.

Making sure that all guests leave the reception safely and sorting out any last minute taxis if necessary.

After the big day, if the bride and groom would like to do so, the best man may place a marriage announcement in the newspaper.

The Chief Bridesmaid

The chief bridesmaid – traditionally called a maid of honour (unmarried) or matron of honour (married) – is usually a close friend or sister of the bride.

She is the main sounding-board in the lead-up to the wedding and on the day itself. She must be a confidante and a trustworthy friend; it is important that she understands the idiosyncrasies of the bride.

She is the bride's main helper. This will include involvement in plans before the wedding and acting as her key aide on the day. She must keep the bride calm and ensure that she is getting ready according to schedule, checking that she has everything she needs and helping her with her dress.

DUTIES BEFORE THE DAY

※ Clarifying with the bride how much involvement she will have in the lead-up to and on the wedding day.

※ Attending wedding dress fittings, if required, and helping to assemble the accessories and going-away outfit. Assisting the bride with the choice of dresses for the bridesmaids.

※ Acting in a support role if there are any strained relations between the bride and her parents, or between the bride and groom.

※ Organising a suitable hen night or weekend, tailored to the bride's wishes and tastes.

※ Keeping in close contact with the best man and other adult bridesmaids (if there are any); liaising with the parents of any young bridesmaids and pageboys.

※ Attending the rehearsal and introducing herself to anyone she hasn't met before.

DUTIES ON THE DAY

※ First and foremost, being a calm and collected presence, who will reassure the bride.

※ Helping the bride into her dress and being with her while her hair and make-up is done.

※ Keeping hold of any make-up or necessities required for touch-ups or unseen eventualities during the day.

※ Ensuring that any small bridesmaids or pageboys are calm and dressed on time and that they know what they have to do. A secret stash of goodies (e.g. non-sugary treats) is a good idea.

※ Escorting the bridal party into the cars and waiting with them outside the ceremony venue for the bride.

※ Once the bride has stepped out of the car, helping to arrange her dress, veil and bouquet. Keeping an eye on the back of her dress and arranging/adjusting her train. Lining everyone up to walk down the aisle.

※ Taking the bride's bouquet during the ceremony, and handing it back to her before she is ready to walk out. Putting back her veil, if requested.

※ Exiting the venue on the arm of the best man, and escorting the bridesmaids and pageboys to the reception.

※ Communicating with the best man throughout the day to ensure that everything is running smoothly.

※ Keeping a constant eye on the bride, and making sure she has everything she needs.

※ Assisting the bride when she is changing into her going-away outfit.

Adult Bridesmaids

Some brides prefer to have children as their bridesmaids while others like to enlist the help of their close girlfriends. It is a matter of personal choice: younger brides often opt for adults, while older brides usually have friends with children and therefore choose younger bridesmaids. Many brides choose a combination of adults and children.

Adult bridesmaids are usually the bride's closest friends. They are generally assistants to the bride and the chief bridesmaid; their level of involvement will vary depending on the size of the wedding and the wishes of the bride.

The bridesmaids will have a say in the choice of dresses and accessories – they must be available for shopping trips and fittings. They will also be involved in organising the hen party.

On the day, the bridesmaids help out with last minute preparations, and sometimes assist the bride in dressing. The chief bridesmaid delegates any tasks.

If there are child bridesmaids and pages, the bridesmaids must look after them before and during the service, see them into the wedding cars, assemble them for photographs, and round them up when the speeches are about to start. If there is only one child bridesmaid or pageboy, the chief bridesmaid should choose one adult bridesmaid to look after the child as required.

The bridesmaids help the chief bridesmaid to get the bride ready before the ceremony begins. They participate in the procession and recessional.

At the reception, the bridesmaids must circulate and talk to all the guests. They should keep an eye on proceedings and report any problems or difficulties to the chief bridesmaid and best man.

Baby Bridesmaids and Pageboys

Child bridesmaids or pageboys are often nieces, nephews, cousins, godchildren, or offspring from a previous marriage. Their purpose is, fundamentally, aesthetic. Practically, they have very little to do other than look sweet and follow the bride down the aisle in the procession and the recessional.

Children under four are generally too young for the role. No one can predict how children will behave on the day, but excitable children never make ideal bridesmaids or pages. On the day, the parents should keep an eye on their child and take responsibility for them whenever this is necessary.

If there are jobs that the bride wishes the children to do – such as handing out confetti – then the chief bridesmaid or another adult bridesmaid can be briefed in advance to oversee things.

Flower girls are an alternative to bridesmaids. They walk down the aisle ahead of the bride, scattering petals, and then sit with their parents before joining the recessional.

THINGS TO CONSIDER

❋ It should be explained to the child that their part in the day is important, and they should be aware that it is an honour to be chosen. They must understand what they will be expected to do, which will save last minute nerves or surprises.

❋ It is a good idea for the child to attend the rehearsal so that the setting and people are familiar on the day.

❋ The child's parents could be asked to promise their child a reward for good behaviour on the day, such as a longed-for yet inexpensive present that is given as soon as the service and photographs are finished.

❋ An adult bridesmaid should take charge of the younger ones. During the service, bribery using small toys or even treats can rescue most situations. Be sure to choose something stain-free, such as plain boxes of mini-raisins and water rather than chocolate or juice, and remember that sweets might make children even more excitable.

❋ One way of catering for children at the reception is to create a children's-only table and a separate area where they can be looked after, perhaps with the help of a magician or entertainer.

❋ Alternatively, they can be seated at tables alongside their parents, but possibly served a children's menu.

❋ Goody bags are a wise investment. Contents can include non-staining coloured pencils and drawing books, or quiet toys. In summer, bubble machines keep children entertained, as well as looking festive.

The Ushers

Good friends or relatives of the groom are usually chosen to be ushers, often along with a relative of the bride, such as her brother. A chief usher can also be nominated to work closely with the best man.

The ushers are the floor managers on the day, in charge of crowd control and generally helping out. They must assist the best man with his duties and are the first faces guests will see when they arrive for the ceremony.

Before the big day, the ushers' only duties are to ensure that they have a suitable outfit to wear – usually already owned or specifically hired – and to attend the stag night. On the day, they are expected to help make things run smoothly and efficiently. If the bridesmaids need any help, they may call on the ushers too.

The best man (and groom if he chooses to) should brief the ushers in advance, including the order of service, the reserved seating plan, any car parking or transport logistics, the procedure at the reception and rough timings of the day.

Ushers should all have their mobile phones with them on the day, and the chief usher should also have a list of contact numbers for key people, such as the chief bridesmaid, groom, caterer and venue manager, just in case of emergency. It is a good idea to have a car on standby for last minute drop-offs or collections.

Ushers are not off-duty once the ceremony is over; they are expected to be ambassadors for the groom, ready to help out throughout the day and evening.

DUTIES ON THE DAY

▨ Making sure there is a stack of umbrellas in the church in case it rains; unpatterned ones look best in wedding photographs. Ensuring that there are two umbrella stands for guests' brollies – something other than a black bin.

▨ Collecting the buttonholes and order of service sheets and distributing them.

▨ Not drinking too much before the ceremony and arriving at the ceremony venue at least 45 minutes in advance.

▨ Handing out the order of service sheets to guests when they arrive and leading them to their seats.

▨ If the venue is filling up on one side and not the other, ensuring that the crowd is balanced out.

▨ Placing a set of order of service sheets at the front for the bridal party.

▨ Letting guests know, on arrival, about any photographic or confetti restrictions.

▨ If the weather is exceptionally hot, having small bottles of water to hand. If it's very cold, having a few blankets to hand for the elderly and children.

▨ Escorting the groom's parents and the mother of the bride to their seats.

▨ Keeping an eye on the door so that one of them can indicate to the best man that the bride has arrived.

▨ Ensuring that the guests move from the ceremony to the reception efficiently, and that they know where to go.

▨ Collecting the pew end flowers to place on the backs of the wedding party's chairs at the reception.

▨ At the reception, helping guests find their tables, ensuring that those who come on their own or need to be looked after have drinks.

The Roles of the Parents

The parents of both the bride and groom have important roles to play. Their level of involvement in the build-up to the wedding and on the day depends, to a great extent, on who is paying for the wedding. The relationship between the bride and her parents and, in turn, their relationship with their future son-in-law is also a deciding factor.

It is worth remembering what was done in the parents' day was very different from the more lavish weddings most couples now choose. The bride and groom have to be accommodating and compromise in certain situations, especially if they are financially dependent on the parents for the wedding, but they must remember that it is their wedding day. In extreme cases, they may have to control the parents' level of involvement.

If the bride and groom are paying for their own wedding, the parents' level of involvement is decided by the bride and groom and can be, if they wish, simplified to traditional roles and attendance on the day.

THE MOTHER OF THE BRIDE

It is a memorable experience for mothers and daughters to organise a wedding. Traditionally, the mother of the bride plays a hugely influential and prominent role.

The bride should establish how much she wants her mother to do; she can take some of the pressure off the bride by attending meetings and making appointments.

If the bride's mother is hosting the wedding, especially from her home, then her level of involvement is high. Alongside the bride, she is in charge of most of the organisation and is the point of contact for suppliers. This role will often include arranging everything from venue or marquee hire, to flower meetings and dress fittings. She may also be asked to send out the invitations and manage the responses.

On the day, the mother of the bride helps, if required, with the dressing and usually accompanies the bridesmaids to the ceremony. She is the last to be seated before the bride's entrance, and is accompanied down the aisle to her seat on the arm of the chief usher. She sits, with the father of the bride or whoever is chosen to give the bride away, on the left of the aisle, usually signs the register and then joins the recessional on the arm of the groom's father.

Once at the reception, she is a co-host, responsible for welcoming guests, circulating and making introductions. Traditionally, the bride's parents do not leave the wedding reception until the last guests have gone, but this is unnecessary if the party ends in the small hours.

THE FATHER OF THE BRIDE

If he is hosting the wedding with the bride's mother, then he is usually aware of the arrangements, and may choose to participate in some aspects of the organisation. Traditionally, he provides a budget and runs the finances of the wedding.

On the day, he and the bride have a little time alone before travelling together to the ceremony. He accompanies her in the car to the ceremony, and walks her down the aisle on his right arm. When the vicar/registrar asks, 'who is giving this woman to this man?', he takes the bride's right hand and places it in the vicar/registrar's.

He sits to the left of the aisle, usually with the mother of the bride, and attends the signing of the register. He takes the bridegroom's mother on his right arm, and escorts her down the aisle during the recessional.

If he is co-hosting the reception, he welcomes guests and, traditionally, when the speeches are announced, he is called to speak first.

THE GROOM'S PARENTS

The groom's parents can be involved as much as they are invited to be, or wish to be. Again, this may depend upon the financial support they are offering. Traditionally, the groom's mother's role is limited, but she is often involved and kept updated.

In the case of the reception being held at their house, or the bride having strained parental relations or no parents still living, then the dynamic changes completely and the groom's parents will often assume the roles traditionally fulfilled by the bride's parents.

On the day, they sit in the second pew/row of seats on the right, and join the recessional. The groom's father escorts the mother of the bride out down the aisle, and the groom's mother is usually escorted by the father of the bride.

DIVORCED PARENTS

This is a sensitive area that has to be addressed right from the start. It is best to keep everything in the open and avoid secrets. Every case will be very different and depends on how the bride and groom mediate the situation. If there are tensions between children, parents and step-parents, it is important that the bride and groom outline roles at an early stage so that everyone is aware of the part they will play on the wedding day.

Unless relations are so strained that the only solution is not to invite one of the parties involved, duties should be split. For example, the natural father could walk the bride down the aisle and the stepfather could give a speech. Prominence is often accorded to the party that brought up the bride.

Forward planning is vital when it comes to seating arrangements for the ceremony and lunch/dinner and the line-ups in official photographs.

BRIDE
TO BE

Choosing the Wedding Dress

Once the date and location of the wedding have been decided, the bride must start looking for her dress. It's best to start as soon as possible as it can take longer than expected. On average, dresses take six months to be made; the bride is usually asked to attend several fittings.

If the bride is unsure where to start, she should go to a department store where a range of designers can be found under one roof. She can work out her preferences and desired style before going to a specific designer. Many department stores, however, only cater for brides who fit within regular sizes.

Bridal shops require appointments. Evenings and weekends get taken quickly, so book up well in advance. Some shops may require a payment to secure a weekend

appointment. January to March tend to be the busiest months, as most brides prefer to get married in the spring or summertime.

The bride must be realistic about her budget, setting an upper and lower limit and sticking to it. Alteration and fitting costs should be borne in mind. Underwear, shoes, headpieces and jewellery may also have to come out of the same budget. The bridal shop will usually ask the bride what her budget is to ensure that she is trying on affordable dresses.

The style of wedding day and the venue should have been decided upon before the bride begins the process of choosing her dress. Different dresses fit different styles of day, be it country, city, vintage or contemporary.

BUYING THE DRESS

The bride should listen to the assistant – they will be familiar with their own dresses and know what suits different figures. She must be open-minded and experiment with all sorts of styles – dresses on a hanger may look surprisingly different when they are actually tried on. Many brides end up choosing something very different to what they originally imagined.

Some brides undertake the search on their own. Others go with their mother or chief bridesmaid. It is a good idea not to attend fittings with too many people, as the bride may end up feeling swamped by conflicting opinions, cramped and indecisive. In general, wedding shops do not encourage large groups.

The bride should stop the search when two or three possible dresses have been found, and then try them on again before making her final choice. Putting on a well-structured wedding dress should be a transformative process. It will feel unlike ordinary clothes and will change the bride's posture and bearing.

Bridal shops normally work in two ways. If the bride is an average size and shape, and after being measured naturally falls into one of the usual dress sizes (i.e. 12, 14 etc.), the shop will make her a standard sized dress that is then tailored for her. Alternatively, if she is a more unusual shape and doesn't comfortably fall into an average size (e.g. very long legs, a short body, small waist and big hips), then a made-to-measure dress will be needed; this is often more expensive.

Once the dress has been chosen, the shop will require a deposit – normally 50 per cent of the total cost. The balance will be due on the day of collection, but expected alteration costs must be talked through at this point. Alterations are often charged by the hour and can really add up. Shops may offer a staggered payment option to make more expensive dresses affordable.

There will be subsequent fittings; the number and timing of these depend on the shop. The bride must wear her wedding underwear and shoes to the final fitting. The veil and other accessories are chosen last.

The Style of the Dress

CONSIDERATIONS

While a full length dress is traditional, a bride may choose a mid-calf or knee-length dress; this will depend on the theme and style of the wedding as a whole.

Skin tone must be taken into account. Ivory is generally the most flattering; white can look harsh against the skin. Cream, pale gold and even cappuccino can work well with some skin tones. It is worth paying extra for high quality fabrics; they are more comfortable and sit well.

PRACTICALITIES

It is a good idea to practise putting on the dress and accessories in advance. The dress shop should advise on the correct order for dressing and fastening everything.

Cotton gloves must be worn when handling it; no one should wear shoes near the dress until the last minute. Never get the dress professionally steamed. Instead, hang it up in the bathroom.

STYLES AND BODY SHAPES

The bride must always choose a dress that suits her body shape, rather than opting for something she adores that does not do her justice.

A-line, with a narrow bodice and a skirt that flares from the waist, is good for big hips.

Ballerina has full netting and usually a tulle skirt, which is good for hourglass figures, but can swamp more petite brides.

Bias is cut on the cross and is suitable for tall and slim figures, but not good for pear shapes.

Empire, with a v-neck or straps and a main seam below the bust, is good for big busts. It can also create an illusion of height.

Princess has a gentle flare from below the bust and is good for pear shaped figures.

Column dresses hang straight and are unforgiving on fuller figures. They are only really suitable for brides who are tall and slim.

A two-piece bodice and skirt is a practical and adaptable style when the bride's top and bottom are different sizes.

Big busts: avoid over-ornamentation and excessive fabric on the bust. Strapless dresses are not advisable either. Good underwear is essential; v- or scalloped necklines are flattering.

Petites: short legs can be elongated by a high waisted dress. Small waists and busts can be emphasised by a fitted bodice; this will also improve posture.

TRAINS

There are three main styles of train: duster, the smallest that just sweeps the floor; puddle, which is prominent but manageable with a little help from the bridesmaids; and cathedral, which is excessively long and very difficult to manage.

The chief bridesmaid should practise lifting and arranging the train so that she can easily set it up before the bride walks up the aisle and for the photographs.

Trains can be gathered up and fixed to the dress with buttons, forming a kind of draped bustle later on in the day. This will allow the bride to walk and dance without having to worry about a dragging train. They are also sometimes lifted up and out of the way using a set of ribbons. Either way, a flattering bustle-like gathering of fabric is created at the back of the dress.

Underwear

Good underwear is an essential investment for the wedding day. The style of dress and the bride's figure dictate what pieces must be worn. The bridal underwear must be worn for final dress fittings.

Structured dresses – for example those with bodices – may not require a bra because support will be built in. Other dresses require good fitting underwear to create the smooth foundations necessary for a perfect and flattering line.

Thin, body-clinging fabrics require nude, seam free, invisible underwear. Visible pant lines must be avoided – either by wearing control pants or thongs – especially as the congregation will be looking at the back of the bride during the ceremony.

Basques can provide a good lift, while also holding in the stomach. A backless basque that fastens below the waist is a good option for low backed or backless dresses. They are available off the peg or, more expensively, to order.

Suspender belts and stockings only work with dresses that have fuller skirts, a lining or under-skirts, otherwise they can show through. Traditionally the bride wears a garter, depending on the cut of the dress. There are varying styles and types, but brides often find a little detail on the garter a useful way of wearing something 'blue', as is tradition.

If practical but unaesthetic knickers must be worn, the bride can change into a more attractive pair before she leaves for her wedding night.

Jewellery and Accessories

JEWELLERY

Many brides borrow a striking piece of jewellery for the wedding day. Nothing, however, should detract from the bride's face. The more ornate the dress, the less jewellery is needed. Plainer dresses, on the other hand, often suit a more decorative piece.

No rings, apart from the engagement ring, should be worn. On the wedding day, the engagement ring is worn on the bride's right hand, leaving her finger ready for the wedding ring. She then puts her engagement ring back on her left hand after the ceremony.

The neckline of the dress and the hairstyle – up or down – must be considered. Necklaces must hang well, sit flat and complement the shape of the neckline.

Jewellery must be carefully chosen with the wedding dress in mind and, if in doubt, brides are advised to err on the classic side.

※ Earrings should be simple and chosen to suit the bride's hairstyle. Be cautious of large, dangly earrings, especially if wearing a veil.

※ Bracelets must be light and simple. They should not detract from the bouquet or the engagement and wedding rings.

※ Most brides choose not to wear a watch.

※ Brooches can be used to accessorise, and are effective when pinned to a sash or gathered seam on the dress.

HEADDRESSES

A headdress or headpiece is often chosen as an alternative to a veil, and can only be designed or bought once the dress has been chosen.

A family piece, such as a tiara, can be borrowed for the day. Make sure it has been professionally cleaned (if necessary) and tried on with the wedding dress.

The headdress is an item where the bride can introduce some individuality – if it suits her character and the style of her dress.

It must be comfortable, secure and must look good from all angles. Anything too heavy or difficult to fasten is not a good idea.

It should be taken along to the run-through with the hairdresser. This will enable the hairdresser to experiment with fitting the headdress before the big day. If a bespoke piece is being made, then the bride will need at least two fittings – one with the dress.

TRADITIONS

Something old, something new
Something borrowed, something blue

Something old: this is traditionally a garter given to the bride by a happily married woman. Many brides opt for a piece of jewellery or a family heirloom such as a tiara.

Something new: this symbolises the newly-weds' happy and prosperous future. This can be anything from the dress or shoes to the veil or headpiece.

Something borrowed: an item such as jewellery is often lent by the bride's family. Alternatively, the chief bridesmaid may lend the bride something of hers. The bride must return the item after the wedding to ensure good luck.

Something blue: many brides choose a garter with a little bit of blue, such as a trimming or appliquéd flower. Alternatively, a piece of blue ribbon can be tied on to the bride's underwear.

Shoes

Shoes must be comfortable and good quality. The bride should not have to worry about her feet rubbing or hurting on the day. She should be prepared to pay a considerable amount in order to guarantee comfort.

FABRIC
Silk or satin shoes are usually worn; leather looks harsh against the soft fabrics of a wedding dress. They can easily be dyed to match the colour of the dress fabric.

SHAPE
The bride should remember that the front of the shoe will be noticed the most, so she should choose the shape carefully, and decide on open or closed toes.

HEELS
Shoes with a heel improve posture and make the bride walk more slowly and, therefore, elegantly. They must not be too high, however, as the bride will be on her feet all day and should not have to worry about comfort and balance. Small, kitten-style heels are a good option.

FLATS
The bride may not want to appear taller than the groom. She should consider flat shoes, such as court shoes or ballet pumps, if this might be a problem.

WEAR
Bridal shoes should be worn in around the house; the wedding day should never be the first time they are put on. They must be worn in with extreme care; putting a clean pair of socks over the shoes will protect delicate fabrics. Shoes with leather or smooth soles should be scored to prevent slipping.

FITTINGS
Shoes must be taken along to fittings to ensure that they suit the dress and that the dress is the right length with the heel.

AFTERWARDS
Silk or satin shoes can be dyed after the wedding, providing the bride with a pair of striking shoes for future occasions.

Veils and Cover-Ups

It is only possible to decide whether a veil should be worn once the dress has been chosen. This is purely a matter of personal choice, not convention.

A veil must complement – not compete with – the style of the bride's dress and hair.

Veils can be worn long or short: to the shoulder, elbow, three-quarter or full-length. Veils that fall below the shoulders are the most manageable; they must always be longer than the bride's hair.

The style of the dress will dictate the fabric of the veil. Soft fabrics look the most elegant. A few pearls, crystals or beads to catch the light can make a veil more interesting; a silk ribbon trim can provide definition.

Family or vintage veils often fade, making them difficult to match to a new dress. Professional cleaning can help, but it is best for the bride to take the veil along to dress fittings to check that it matches.

PRACTICALITIES

The veil should be attached to a comb for easy removal; it is a good idea to cross two hairgrips in the bride's hair and attach the comb to them to prevent the veil from slipping.

Ensure that the chief bridesmaid knows how and when to remove the veil after the ceremony.

It is important to see how the veil looks from all angles, on and off the face. The congregation will see it from behind; the groom from the front and side.

Whoever is chosen to lift the veil back during the ceremony (the mother or chief bridesmaid) should have practised a few times before the big moment.

COVER-UPS

Brides who want to wear a strapless dress in church
should cover their shoulders. A longer veil can do this, or
else a cover-up is required. Winter brides will also need
one to prevent shivering and goose pimples.

The wedding dress will dictate the style and type of
fabric used; corded lace, organza, silk and fake fur are
popular choices.

In summer, if the weather is warm, the cover-up is only
required for the church or ceremony. The bride can take
it off after the ceremony and have bare shoulders or a
bare back during the reception. Cover-ups thus provide
the bride with two completely different looks: a formal
one in the church, followed by something more relaxed
and revealing at the reception.

In cooler months, the bride may need to wear her cover-
up all day. Small jackets are popular, and often made
from the same material as the dress to match it perfectly.
Weather considerations will be discussed from the outset
when choosing the dress.

Fake fur stoles are popular with winter or Christmas
brides. They are a good idea for the times of day when
the bride is outside, for example when formal
photographs are being taken, but a lighter, more practical
cover-up may be needed for the reception.

Many brides wear a pashmina-style wrap that matches
the dress around their shoulders. This is a flexible choice,
which can be put on or discarded at will.

The other adult bridesmaids should also consider a cover-
up, such as a wrap, especially if they are wearing strapless
dresses and the weather is chilly. These can be left at the
reception venue in advance if they are only to be used at
the end of the evening.

Hair

When choosing a hairstyle, the bride should think about her hair type, face shape, the line of her dress and the veil or headpiece, if she is wearing one. Her head will be viewed from the back and sides, as well as the front, so the style must look good from every angle.

STYLE

The more intricate the dress, the simpler the hair should be, and vice versa. There are three basic styles to consider: leaving it down, an 'up do' or half-up-half-down. Softer styles, with some loose pieces framing the face, often look flattering. The style must not allow hair to fall into the eyes or fall forward inconveniently onto the face.

The bride must feel that she has a non-restrictive style that she can 'wear' all day. Many brides make the mistake of choosing a style they would never normally wear, and

then regretting it when the pictures come back. It is difficult to establish what type of hair-do or accessories will look best until the dress has been chosen. Hair practice appointments should be booked once the entire outfit has been decided upon.

PROFESSIONALS

Ask for a personal recommendation; the hairdresser must be used to doing 'wedding hair'. Work out how many heads – other than the bride's – need to be dressed on the day and how long is needed for each person. Establish whether the hairdresser will come to the bride on the morning of the wedding (the preferred option), or whether she needs to go to the salon (which may cause logistical problems).

REHEARSAL

The bride should have one or two practice sessions. She should take along photographs or cuttings of styles she likes, and wear a top with a similar line to the dress. She must also take along the headdress and tiara – and jewellery if possible – that have been chosen; this will help with developing the style and checking that it all works together. It is a good idea to take a photograph after the practice session, and again a few hours later, to check the longevity of the style.

The bridesmaids should not need a hair rehearsal, but the hairdresser will want to discuss their style in advance and may want to meet them to see their hair types.

PREPARATION

The bride is advised not to experiment with a new style or colour for at least three months before the wedding; on the day, her hair should be enhanced rather than totally unrecognisable. Hair should be allowed to grow well in advance if the bride is sure she wants her hair up. The bride must not wash her hair on the day if it is being put up as certain styles and slides may not hold.

Grooming and Make-Up

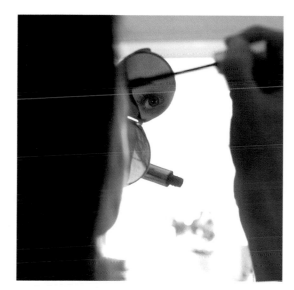

To ensure that the bride looks her best, it is advisable to hire a professional make-up artist for the day. They must be booked well in advance; check prices and terms. A professional can also make up the mother of the bride and adult bridesmaids. Alternatively, make-up counters in department stores offer trials and can give good tips to brides who decide to do their own.

PRACTICE

A trial run is advisable. Wear a top that is similar in style to the top of the wedding dress. The make-up artist will also need to know what style of hair and accessories have been decided upon. The bride must talk through exactly what she wants with her make-up advisor – cuttings from magazines, photographs and so on are all useful. She should take a photograph as soon as it is done (and then again a few hours later) as a reminder.

If possible, the wedding make-up can be decided upon before the hen night, and the make-up artist, or bride herself, can use the hen night as a trial run for the look.

LOOKING NATURAL

Never try something new or experiment on the day itself. Keep the look as natural as possible, and avoid dark lips and false eyelashes. Wearing a lot of make-up won't make it stay on; it will just look too heavy. Waterproof mascara is a good idea for tearful brides.

Make-up should always be applied in natural daylight.

NAILS

Nails must be well manicured as the bride's hands will be the focus of everyone's attention. If nails are very badly bitten, then false nails – done by a highly recommended professional to ensure they look natural – should be considered.

BROWS AND WAXING

Waxing should be up to date and ready for the wedding night and honeymoon. Facials and eyebrow shaping should be done at least a week before the wedding to give the skin time to settle. Eyebrows can always be tamed and touched up on the day.

FAKE TAN

Fake tan looks good on holiday, but very artificial against a wedding dress. The bride must avoid looking overly tanned next to her groom and attendants, which will show up in the photographs. If fake tan is desired, it must be applied professionally and the bride should have had a couple of trial runs beforehand.

TOUCH UP

Brides may wish to restore their make-up as the day goes on; this is a duty for the chief bridesmaid – she must not make drastic changes but just keep the bride looking fresh-faced. Ensure that the make-up she carries is the same brand and colours as those applied by the make-up artist. Sometimes, the make-up artist will supply a 'touching-up' kit for the day on request.

The Bride's Bouquet

The bouquet completes the bride's look and must complement the wedding dress. The more intricate the dress, the simpler the flowers should be, and vice versa.

The colour of the bouquet must fit in with the wedding scheme, and should coordinate with the bridesmaids' dresses, the flowers at the ceremony and the reception.

The shape of the bouquet should reflect the style of the dress, as well as complementing the line of the dress. It should be in proportion to the bride's height and weight.

A sleek fitted dress suits a tapering style of bouquet; a larger skirt suits a rounder one. Tall brides should choose longer bouquets, whereas petite brides may opt for smaller versions.

CHOICES

Timing is important; most florists need to be booked at least six months in advance for summer weddings.

The budget should be discussed early on so that the florist is sure that they are recommending flowers within the right price range.

It is best to keep flowers simple; some of the most stunning bouquets consist of only one or two types of bloom. Those that include many different types can look messy and lose impact.

The bride may wish to hold just one stem, have a bouquet of only one type of flower, or choose a combination of several types of bloom.

Discuss ideas with the florist. Write down any thoughts in advance and take along a swatch of the dress fabric and any magazine cuttings that have inspired and caught the bride's eye.

The choice of flowers is entirely personal. The bride will need to take into account the rate at which they wilt, the time of year and the chosen theme for the day.

The flowers the bride chooses for the bouquet must fit with the general style and setting of the wedding. For example, peonies and English roses can suit the country, whereas lilies, orchids and sculptural tropical stems are more appropriate for a city wedding.

She must make sure she likes the scent of the flowers and steer clear of anything too pollen heavy.

Bouquets can be made up of flowers alone, but will often include a little greenery. A matching single stem can then be used to make buttonholes for the groom, best man, ushers, and fathers.

HOLDING THE BOUQUET

The bouquet should be held at hip-height. Many brides make the mistake of holding it too high, which spoils the line of the dress.

Ensure that a proper grip can be obtained and that it is comfortable to hold. Most florists wrap the holding place/wire with satin ribbon, but grosgrain is a good alternative, as it is less slippery.

CONFETTI

Many ceremony venues will have restrictions on confetti. Metallic confetti is usually totally banned, and many venues dislike paper as it looks so unsightly afterwards. The dye can also seep into bridal fabrics if it gets wet.

A good alternative is to use real flower petals. There are specialist companies offering petals from all sorts of flowers in many different colours.

Baby bridesmaids can hand these out in a basket, or small cones of petals can be distributed to guests.

Seasonal Flowers

Virtually every flower imaginable can be obtained at any time of year from abroad, so the bride is free to choose whatever she wants. It is recommended, however, that the bride decides to use seasonal flowers; they will be fresher and less expensive.

SPRING

Narcissi, Tulips, Muscari, Cherry Blossom, Honeysuckle, Cymbidium Orchid, Lily of the Valley.

SUMMER

Peonies, Hydrangea, Garden Rose, Gardenia, Freesia, Iris, Sweet Pea, Lavender, Cornflower.

AUTUMN

Alstromeria, Dahlia, Antique Rose, Phalaenopsis Orchid, Lisianthus, Michaelmas Daisy.

WINTER

Amaryllis, Snowdrop, English Arium, Velvet Rose, Mistletoe, Snowberry, Winter Jasmine.

AFTERWARDS

Traditionally, the bride tosses her bouquet into the crowd; the single woman who catches it is believed to have received some of the bride's good fortune, and will be the next to marry. If the bride wants to hold on to her bouquet as a keepsake, the catcher may be willing to give it back, she could remove a few stems to dry or some brides have a spare bouquet made up especially to throw.

The bouquet can be preserved after the wedding by hanging it upside down in a dark place. There are also specialist companies who professionally preserve the bouquet by freeze-drying.

Planning the Hen Party

It is often difficult to come up with an imaginative and tasteful hen party idea that is sensitive to everybody's budget. The number one rule is that the hen party is an opportunity to spoil the bride, laugh, relax and have fun. Efficient forward planning will ensure that the event goes with a swing.

THE BASICS

Traditionally, the party is organised by the chief bridesmaid, with help from the bridesmaids and close friends. The bride should supply a list of her friends and their contact details, and give a few hints about what she'd like from the occasion. Remember that taking the bride out of her comfort zone on this momentous occasion might be ill advised.

Tradition dictated that the chief bridesmaid should organise a dinner party at her house, followed by the inevitable move to somewhere more lively. More recently, lavish weekends away came into vogue, with costs escalating and a competitive atmosphere prevailing. Today, anything goes. If the bride opts for a night of uninhibited revelry, rather than a quiet dinner party, that is her choice.

The hen party is a perfect excuse for a girls-only holiday. Where time and budget allow, extending the hen night to a hen weekend, or even further, means that the proceedings can be more relaxed.

TIMING

It is very unusual nowadays for parties to take place the night before the wedding day. Consider holding the hen party four to six weeks before the wedding.

The hen party often takes place at the same time as the stag night – a good idea, if for no other reason than it will keep the bride busy and ensure that she doesn't spend too much time worrying about the fate that may have befallen her fiancé.

GUESTS

Only wedding guests should be invited, and family invitations are a matter of personal choice. Often mothers who accept the invitation make a getaway after the more genteel part of the evening.

It is quite likely that many of the guests at a hen party won't have met before, and the party should be an opportunity for the girls to get to know each other. The bride should act as the bridge between her friends.

Inviting male friends is obviously not the traditional thing to do, but if the bride wants to include her best male friends, it is totally acceptable and her prerogative.

FINANCES

The organiser must budget carefully. Costs should be shared equally among all the guests and should include the bride's share. The budget of every guest should be considered; an expensive weekend away may mean that some guests have to decline. The cost of travel, accommodation, food, entertainment and contributions to presents, outfits or games must be taken into account.

A breakdown of costs can be emailed to guests, who should confirm their contribution. This should be sent promptly so that all guests are aware of these early on.

It is not customary to give the bride a present, though it has become increasingly common. It may be an item that all the guests have contributed to which can be bought in advance. Alternatively, something more personal can be conjured up. A beautiful box containing one item of personal relevance from each friend attending the party is a wonderful gesture.

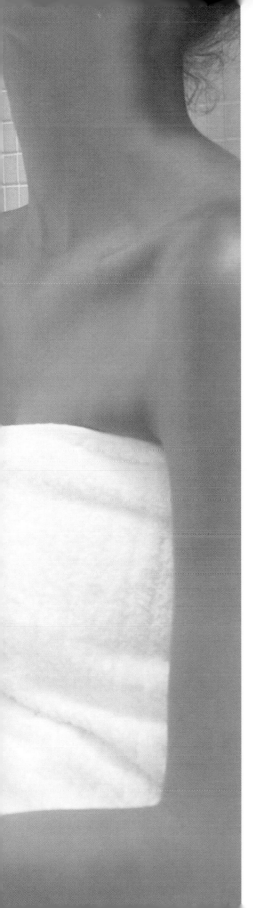

Party Ideas

Any kind of hen night is possible, but be aware that this is, first and foremost, a celebration for the bride, and that her personality and taste must prevail.

A dinner party at home, with caterers, or in a private room at a restaurant.

An evening concert in the park with a candlelit picnic.

A road trip to the seaside or country with cosy pubs, walks, a treasure hunt and a rented cottage to stay in.

A make-over and then big night out to bars and a club.

Breakfast or tea at the most desirable hotel in town.

A lesson of some kind – belly dancing, salsa, wine tasting or jewellery making.

A trip to a spa with fantastic treatments.

A sleepover with vintage movies, manicures, popcorn, ice cream and champagne.

A relaxing beach holiday in the sun with close friends.

A city break in a place where there's lots to see.

A soft adventure activity day – riding, sailing or yoga.

STAG PARTIES

The groom's stag party is organised by the best man, with the help of the ushers and friends. Like the hen party, celebrations should be tailored to the groom's tastes. Whether it's an evening out or a weekend away, nowadays anything goes. It is sensible for the details of the stag and hen parties to be kept a secret from the bride and groom to avoid any spoilt surprises.

COSTUME

Groom, Best Man and Ushers

Traditionally, all members of the groom's party – the groom, best man and ushers – follow a set dress code. The fathers of the bride and groom often follow this code as well. The cardinal rule for male members of the wedding party is not to outdo the groom. All members of the groom's party and other guests should be made aware of the dress code.

Morning attire is the traditional dress for weddings. The slightly odd name derives from a time when weddings took place in the morning and gentlemen naturally wore their morning attire.

Despite the increasing trend for weddings to begin in the afternoon and continue into the evening, morning attire remains the accepted British dress code for weddings, although alternatives include suits and black tie.

The suggestions given here regarding bespoke tailoring apply equally to day suits and dinner suits. Note that day suits are a low-key alternative to morning dress, and ideally should be mid-grey, charcoal grey or navy blue.

Black and even white tie dress codes are an import from the USA, and are becoming popular for showy evening weddings in the UK.

MORNING ATTIRE

Morning attire consists of a morning coat, striped trousers, shirt, tie and waistcoat. It is usual to wear a morning coat throughout the day; a change into black tie for the reception should be regarded as the exception rather than the rule. If such a change is required, this should be stated clearly on the invitation.

The morning coat is single-breasted with one button, and usually has peaked lapels. Grey is the traditional colour, but black is very popular and perfectly acceptable. Featherweave is the classic option for the material.

Striped trousers come in a variety of styles, to suit various shapes and sizes. It is worth exploring the options to find the most flattering stripe. An alternative to stripes is dogstooth check (also known as spongebag).

Flat fronted trousers give a slimmer look; a pleat down the front works better for thinner builds as it draws attention to the waist. Trousers worn with braces hang better than other styles, but are not absolutely necessary. If braces are worn, they should be made of felt and fitted with buttons.

It is essential to wear a waistcoat. Although grey is the traditional colour to wear under a black morning coat, waistcoats in other plain colours or lightly patterned in soft tones can be elegant alternatives. They should be made of linen, silk or brocade (but note that the latter two options may be too hot during high summer).

The waistcoat may be double-breasted, although a single-breasted waistcoat will look better under the single-breasted coat. The bottom button of a single-breasted waistcoat should always be left undone – the waistcoat must sit below the seam of the trousers. This is often impossible to achieve with standard trousers, so true brace trousers should be worn. Backless waistcoats with elastic under the collar and at the base are cooler for summer weddings but do not look quite as smart as the real thing, so are best avoided.

Ties were originally always black to show formality; a silvery speckled tone later became the favoured colour. Today there is no rule, but softer tones work best aesthetically and loud garish varieties are highly discouraged. Stocks and cravats may be worn instead, with a pin.

Many grooms choose to have their party's waistcoats and ties specially made for the occasion. The key colours of

the wedding should be picked out – reflecting the bride's dress, flowers, or a particular colour theme that is being used throughout the day.

Morning attire should be worn with a plain shirt in a pale colour such as white, cream, blue or pink. Traditionally shirts were always white with a stiff, turned down detachable collar, but this is down to personal choice and quite formal by today's standards. Ideally the shirt should have double cuffs and be worn with cufflinks. Most grooms choose to buy a new shirt for the occasion of their wedding.

ACCESSORIES

Shoes are an important consideration: they finish the look off. Black lace-ups with minimal decoration should be worn – the Oxford toecap is the ideal option. Loafers can appear too informal. Socks should be black or grey.

Top hats should be worn on the front of the head; when indoors, they are carried under the arm. The wearer should know how to 'doff' their hat – in other words, raise it above the head to greet guests. Black silk is the ultimate choice, but such hats have not been made since the 1950s. The purchaser of a second hand model should be prepared to pay handsomely. Grey felt is the alternative, and is perfectly acceptable.

Gloves (always grey) tend not to be worn nowadays.

Flowers worn in the buttonhole of the coat/jacket (referred to simply as 'buttonholes') should match colour themes. Often, the groom's buttonhole matches the bride's flowers, and the best man, ushers' and fathers' buttonholes reflect the bridesmaids' flowers.

Look for a good *boutonnière* fixing under the lapel – this small strip holds the flower stalk in place and keeps the buttonhole upright.

Groom, Best Man and Ushers

TO HIRE OR TO BUY?

As a general rule, the groom will pay for his own attire; these days he is not expected to pay for anyone else. If, for financial reasons, suits are hired, the groom's party may wish to have waistcoats and/or ties specially made.

The most affordable option is to hire. Dedicated shops stock a good range of sizes so it should be relatively easy to find a suit that fits well. Most hire shops offer helpful advice as to fittings and styles. The groom should go in with a clear idea of what he wants and even make a list or take in a picture of the required clothing; if in doubt the best plan is to ask for advice.

The outfit should be reserved well in advance of the day, shops usually ask for a deposit in advance, with the balance payable once delivery has been taken. When the suit is picked up, it should be tried on again to ensure that it is comfortable. The best man or an usher should be appointed to return the groom's outfit after the wedding.

There are various options for buying: bespoke, ex-hire, off-the-peg. Bespoke suits are the ultimate in luxury: a hand-made suit will fit and flatter perfectly. Although it involves great expense, it should last forever. The groom should allow at least four months for the suit to be made and visit a recommended tailor. There will be at least three fittings.

Ex-hire and off-the-peg suits are more affordable options; they can be altered to fit. Many hire shops offer ex-hire suits for sale. Good second-hand shops often have morning suits in excellent condition on their rails. These can be a good choice as they are built to last.

Owning morning attire can be useful – the cost and fuss of hiring a suit for every wedding one attends in a decade can be astronomical, and may well justify the more expensive option of buying.

KILTS

It is said in some quarters that Scotsmen should not wear tartan south of the border, but that rule has been very much relaxed over the last few decades. Nowadays it is most acceptable to wear tartan, but wearing a kilt when there is no Scottish (or Gaelic) connection might be seen as a rather pretentious gesture.

The groom may wear his own tartan – modern, ancient or dress. The kilt is accompanied by either a short tweed 'day' jacket and matching tweed waistcoat worn with a plain shirt and tie, or a Kenmore velvet jacket and jabot. Kilt hose (never white or cream), garter flashes and *Sgian Dubh* (the dagger) are also worn. The type of jacket dictates the type of sporran to be worn: a leather day sporran sits with the tweed jacket and a dress sporran (probably decorated with fur) accompanies the velvet jacket. The other option is to wear tartan trews with a morning coat.

UNIFORMS

Only active members of the armed forces may wear military uniform; permission to do so should be sought from a commanding officer. Each regiment has its own traditions and protocol for weddings: for instance, in some regiments it is not customary to wear uniform at all, and swords may or may not be worn.

The groom and best man should be dressed in the same style, so a member of the forces who wishes to wear uniform may reconsider if his best man is a civilian. In this case, the groom may wear a regimental tie instead.

A 'guard of honour' may be formed outside the church. If the guard are carrying swords or lances, these will be raised to form an arch, under which the bride and groom will walk upon leaving the church. Again, the traditions and rules of the particular armed service and unit should be researched and adhered to.

Bridesmaids

Sophisticated and elegant, bridesmaids are a complement to the bride but must in no way draw attention away from her. They are most likely to wear a dress or a bodice and skirt. It is imperative to choose outfits that will flatter all figures: a sensible option is to dress the bridesmaids in various styles made in identical material. Creativity can here be blended with traditional form to create an individual, memorable look.

The choice of dress must reflect the style of the wedding: long evening gowns are appropriate for traditional elegance, but more contemporary styles that may be used after the event as party dresses are also a practical option. The choice of colour should fit with the bride's dress and flowers. While the bride has the final say over attire, but she must be willing to be flexible.

COUTURE OR HIGH STREET?

The first port of call is often a specialist shop stocking a wide selection of bridesmaids' dresses. Buying from here can be expensive; alterations will usually be necessary and anything sold in a bridal shop will be priced at a premium. Even if the desired dresses are not found here a trip to a specialist shop offers a perfect opportunity to consider all the style options and gather ideas.

Those ideas can be presented to a good dressmaker. Six months should be allowed for bespoke dresses, with several fittings required. Final measurements will be taken around two months before the wedding day. Ideas for styles are best conveyed by taking along pictures from magazines, or even a dress that a member of the bridal party already owns and would like copied.

Dressmakers can take care of the entire procedure, from finding patterns and fabrics to measuring and fitting; some also organise tights, shoes and hair accessories.

Beautiful and affordable dresses can also be found on the high street. Traditionally the bride's family would pay, but this is not expected. An adult bridesmaid may wish to pay for her own dress.

FLOWERS

Bouquets should be understated and simple, perhaps hand tied singles or small bouquets. A basic version of the bride's bouquet is a safe option, or the bouquet can coordinate with the bridesmaids' dresses and the bride's bouquet. For a more unusual look each bridesmaid may carry different flowers.

SHOES

Bridesmaids spend much of the day on their feet, so comfort is an important consideration. Shoes can be dyed to match dresses. If bridesmaids are different heights, heels can be varied to create a balanced group.

HAIR AND MAKE-UP

Hair and make-up styles, like everything else, should coordinate. An 'updo' for long haired bridesmaids is much smarter than leaving hair down. Matching clips, flowers or slides can help to create a uniform look.

Make-up should be discreet. If time or budget do not allow for this to be done professionally the bride and bridesmaids should visit a reliable make-up counter well before the day to agree on some guidelines. A practice make-up and hair session is advisable.

CONSIDERATIONS

✷ Skin tones should be borne in mind when deciding on colours and fabrics.

✷ Underwear should be planned well in advance and, if possible, worn to the final dress fitting.

✷ Consider the weather and time of year: stoles or shrugs may come in useful for day-to-evening.

Baby Bridesmaids and Pageboys

Traditional dress is a suit or knickerbockers for boys, and a dress for girls. Colours and styles should complement the colour scheme and overall look of the wedding. Many people like to follow themes such as pirates or cowgirls but they do err on the informal side. Comfort and fit are paramount: every possible measure should be taken to ensure that small children are happy in their outfits.

If little girls already own a party dress or bridesmaid's dress that matches the outfits of the bridal party it is perfectly acceptable for them to wear this. A ballerina length skirt with a high waist will suit small girls; ankle or mid-calf length is a sensible choice for girls aged five and above. Fabrics should complement the bride's dress – dupion, satin, organza and chiffon are the most popular choices. All natural fabrics can be dyed after the event and turned into

party dresses. Contrasting or tartan sashes can be used to add a flash of colour.

Pages can wear shirts and Nehru-collared jackets with knickerbockers or short trousers. Older boys might be given the role of honorary usher: a plain or Nehru jacket and flat fronted trousers will suffice. At a wedding with traditional Scottish dress, boys should wear kilts or trews with either a jacket or a smart jersey.

FINDING THE PERFECT OUTFIT

Dresses and outfits can be acquired from specialist companies, or reasonable alternatives can be found on the high street. The bride, her family or the parents of the bridesmaid/page may pay the bill. Sometimes the cost is shared: where a dressmaker is used the parents

might pay for the fabric and the bride for the making up. If bridesmaids or pageboys live at a distance, the chosen dressmaker must be accommodating and willing to do much of the fitting by by post and phone. Mothers can measure their children and ring the details through.

SHOES

Ballet shoes or pumps with rubber soles prevent slipping on wet days. Elastic across the top or ribbons around the ankles will prevent shoes from falling off. Shoes can always be dyed to match dresses. For boys, traditional patent buckle shoes can be hired, but smart lace ups are also fine.

FLOWERS

Getting children to carry flowers and remember to keep hold of them can be tricky, so a pomander with a ribbon around it, attached to the wrist, is a safe choice for girls. Alternatively, a small basket containing flowers or petals that reflect the bride's bouquet or the church flowers can look good. Flowers can also be worn in the hair, fixed to a slide or Alice band. Pages may wear a buttonhole with a miniature version of the groom's flower although they do not necessarily need to carry anything.

An effective alternative is a long ribbon decorated with flowers that match the bridesmaids' bouquets (the florist should be able to take care of this) which all the children hold as they walk down the aisle.

CONSIDERATIONS

※ Children grow at an astonishing rate. Clothes must not be bought too far in advance or they may no longer fit come the wedding day. Dressmakers should also take this into account.

※ Slides and flowers tend to fall out of clean hair; it should be washed the day before and left.

※ Making too much effort to coordinate young children can be a mistake and is likely to look contrived.

※ Make-up should be avoided.

The Parents

MOTHERS

Planning is key – the outfit should be considered and finalised well in advance; a common mistake is leaving it to the last minute when there are so many other things to think about.

Clothes should be comfortable at the same time as having an impact. Many mothers will choose a discreet, elegant outfit and rely on a striking hat to make their appearance truly remarkable. Hats are traditional but by no means compulsory. Many mothers choose to wear something simple and accessorise with beautiful jewellery; though most like to buy a new outfit or have one made, but this is by no means requisite.

The bride and groom's mothers should confer to avoid embarrassing clashes or similarities, and discuss whether or not hats or headpieces are to be worn.

CONSIDERATIONS

✼ A hair and make-up professional will take the pressure off on the day and apply long-lasting make-up.

✼ Overly bright colours and patterns should be avoided as they may overpower photographs, and care should be taken not to overshadow the bride.

✼ Shoes should be comfortable (slightly worn in) and not so high that they will be painful after a few hours.

✼ A shoulder bag is easier to manage than a clutch when juggling a champagne glass and shaking hands. Hats should not hamper kissing.

FATHERS

The fathers of the bride and groom are generally considered as members of the groom's party in terms of attire. Refer to the section on the groom's clothing.

THE PARTY

Hired Venues

Choosing a suitable reception venue is all-important. A good venue will be large enough, well located and will ideally enhance everyone's experience of the wedding, combining good facilities with, for example, a historic building, elegant rooms, beautiful gardens, or a striking view.

Historical properties, although they are frequently subject to restrictions, are popular choices for both ceremonies and receptions. They are a good option for couples having a civil ceremony who seek imposing surroundings. Often, they are large enough for both the ceremony and reception and can accommodate the bride and groom, wedding party and guests overnight.

Religious ceremonies usually require a separate reception venue, but many civil ceremonies are held in the same place as the reception. Whether a venue is required for both the ceremony and reception, or just the reception, finding somewhere suitable can be a daunting task. Popular venues get booked up well in advance – sometimes up to 18 months – especially on summer Saturdays. Anywhere that is near a ceremony venue will be especially popular. The bride and groom, and often a parent or close friend, should look at as many venues as possible before deciding what suits them best.

DECIDING FACTORS

If the reception venue is separate it should, ideally, be close to the ceremony venue. While people will accept that a certain amount of travel is unavoidable, guests should not be expected to travel for more than 30 minutes. Problems with cars, summer traffic jams and navigation can all take the edge off guests' enjoyment.

Venue size is critical. Ideally, there should be separate drinks and dining areas at the reception. If the venue is too small for both, a marquee for the reception drinks or the dinner can be erected.

Hired Venues: Details

RESTRICTIONS

Check out all the venue's restrictions before booking. Some frequent examples are:

※ No flowers prone to causing pollen stains.

※ No red wine (unless the guests are seated).

※ No floor-damaging stilettos.

※ No smoking or candlelight.

※ Limitations on the length of the reception.

※ Monitoring of noise level.

※ Limitations on the age of guests (e.g. young children).

FOOD AND DRINK

Many venues will offer in-house catering. It is vital that the quality of the food is checked before confirming any booking; the couple should organise a canapé and food tasting and discuss the flexibility of the menu.

If the venue's catering proves to be unsatisfactory, then the couple must check whether outside caterers may be brought in and whether they will be allowed to use the kitchen facilities.

Some venues do not provide food themselves, but have a recommended list of suppliers. The bride and groom should contact the suppliers for quotes and check that they fall within their budget.

Finally, the bride and groom should confirm whether alcohol and soft drinks are provided in-house. They should pay careful attention to the choice of wines and the price range of drinks on offer. If they are allowed to supply the drink themselves, it is important to check corkage fees; this is a hidden charge which can add considerably to costs.

PARKING

Sufficient parking for guests and suppliers must be provided. It is a good idea to find out whether non-resident guests are able to leave their cars at the venue overnight. This is a useful facility for guests who have a few drinks and are happy to pick up their vehicles the following day.

AMENITIES

There must be plenty of lavatories (allow one per 40 guests) of a decent standard and accessible to the elderly. It is advisable to request a separate one for the bride, mother of the bride and chief bridesmaid, if they are non-residents; the bride can then touch up her make-up in private and avoid queueing.

Marquees

A marquee is not merely a covered seating area, it provides the bride and groom with a blank canvas on which they can impose their own personalities and style. There are a vast range of structures and interiors to choose from; marquees can be as traditional or contemporary as suits the style of the wedding.

Marquees can be very expensive; follow personal recommendations and obtain a number of quotes. Check that the company actually owns the marquees itself, and is not acting as a sub-contractor. Marquee companies are at their busiest during the summer, and should be booked six to seven months ahead. They can be booked nearer to the event for October to April weddings.

TYPE AND SIZE OF MARQUEE

The marquee should embellish, not obstruct, its surroundings. It should not cover up a beautiful house or garden aspect, but blend in, enhancing the setting.

Frame marquees have the benefit of no guy ropes and can be erected virtually anywhere. Pole and peg marquees vary from classic canvas to Raj tents. They need more space for the guy ropes and, while visually impressive, tend to come in more limited sizes.

The marquee supplier provides a proposed floor plan and works out the size required, based on the couple's requirements and the number of guests. There may also be a bar area and a dance floor; assume that a third to half of your guests will be dancing at any one time.

Be careful not to underestimate the amount of standing room required, as the waiting staff will need space to circulate when serving drinks. Remember to allow room for extras such as the cake table, table for presents and so on. A fine balance must be struck between having enough room for comfort and too much space so that the marquee is lacking in atmosphere.

137

Marquees: Details

FLOORS

There are various options for the floor. An underlying waterproof membrane is essential and matting is an economic option. Hard, levelled cassette flooring gives the most professional finish; it may be essential if the ground is on a slope or very uneven, but it is expensive.

LININGS AND SIDES

Marquee linings range from highly decorative patterns to the standard crinkle lining. There are starlit ceilings – only suitable for evening receptions – different types of windows, and clear sides that will make the marquee feel an integral part of the garden. There will be plenty of colour and interest provided by flowers and table settings, so don't choose too intricate a marquee if there is going to be an elaborate decorative theme.

POWER

A generator and a back-up emergency generator (even if there is a mains supply) are required. The power used by the caterers, lighting and music system is likely to overload a normal domestic system. Generators are large and unwieldy, so it is advisable to choose a sensible place to hide them; make sure the supplier brings extra cabling. Ask for a super-silent generator where possible; a persistent hum can distract from the speeches. The insurance policy should cover the generator – they are very expensive to replace.

Marquee companies will be able to advise on, and supply, lighting: chandeliers, pinspots and uplighters will all add to the party atmosphere, while more specialist lighting effects can be used for the post-dinner dancing.

FURNITURE

Marquee companies will also quote for tables, chairs and linen. There is usually no obligation to use them if the bride and groom are looking for something different.

SAFETY AND ACCESS

Safety and access routes are another consideration. Guy ropes and areas around the catering tent, lavatories and the car park must be well lit to avoid accidents. There will need to be access for the refrigerated catering van to park near to the catering tent and for portable lavatories to be driven to the appointed area.

AMENITIES

The marquee company will recommend a portable lavatory supplier, if required. If the lavatories are to be used the day after the wedding for another party, arrangements should be made for emptying them first thing that morning. Allow one lavatory per 40 guests and an additional one for staff. Ensure that they are located in a place that is accessible by vehicle and preferably close to a water main.

EXTRAS

Provision should also be made for a catering tent. This must be a reasonable size as the caterers will need to prepare, cook and clear dishes on site. The couple should also discuss thermostatically controlled ducted heating, air conditioning options, and lockable doors.

BACK-UP

Many marquee companies include the cost of an on-site attendant in their quote. This is a good back-up; but if the marquee company is very local, and they are happy to be 'on call' with a quick turn around time, an attendant is not necessary.

QUOTES

When quoting, the marquee company, caterer and any other key suppliers should make a site visit on the same day so that they can meet and discuss individual requirements together. The quote must be studied in great detail and explained by the supplier if necessary. Delivery, set-up and dismantling times must be checked, along with travel costs, insurance and damage policies.

The Seating Plan

The seating plan is a critical organisational task when planning the reception. It becomes an increasingly difficult juggling act as complications arise, people drop out and new guests are added. It must never be left to the last minute.

CHOICE OF TABLES

※ 5' round table – seats 8–10

※ 5'6" round table – seats 8–11

※ 6' round table – seats 10–12

The smallest round tables, which seat eight to ten, are the most sociable. The shape of the venue may dictate the shape and size of the tables.

If the bride and groom decide to have a top table, the traditional seating plan (facing the table from left to right) is as follows: chief bridesmaid, the father of the groom, the mother of the bride, the groom, the bride, the father of the bride, the mother of the groom, and then the best man.

This sort of seating arrangement is, however, very formal, and may make the wedding party feel that they are on public display. It is also not very sociable for those seated in a long line. Round tables might be more successful. The bride and groom need not feel obliged to sit with their families, particularly when there are step-parents or difficult family politics involved.

LAYOUT AND PLANNING

A plan of the room should be made first, locating the wedding party's table(s). Important family or guests' tables can then be allocated. Positions for the speeches and cake cutting, and access routes for the caterer and photographer must also be considered.

A piece of paper to represent each table is a good start – cut into shape for round tables and trestle tables. The name of each guest should then be written on a post it note or tag. The tables and guests can then be laid out and moved around.

If possible, each guest should be flanked by a person of the opposite sex. Ideally, one lively couple or person should be located on each table; spread the ushers around. Guests should be able to recognise at least one other person on their table. Many couples choose to mix the generations, though seating plans are most successful when guests are placed at tables with people with whom they share common interests.

DISPLAYS

Tables are numbered or named after something relevant to the bride and groom, such as places they have visited. Each place setting must have a name card; these can be decorative and themed to match the wedding stationery, or in simple calligraphy.

The table plan – a diagram of all the tables with people's names – should be clearly displayed at the entrance to the seating area. For large weddings, two seating plans may be required. Alternatively, little envelopes with each guest's name, containing a card with a table number or name can be laid out in a prominent place. This can create interest and conversation as guests try to establish who is sitting at their table.

PAPERWORK

The caterers must be supplied with a full seating plan, highlighted to indicate those with special dietary needs. They should also be given an envelope per table containing name cards for laying the tables. If there are any late changes, the best man or chief usher can keep the caterers informed. A few contingency name cards must be to hand for new guests and last-minute changes.

Style and Decor

The style of the wedding as a whole should permeate the choice of decoration at the reception. The day should have a feeling of organic unity; the reception is not the place to spring surprises on unsuspecting guests. The dominant wedding colour, which has already been in evidence in the choice of stationery, dress and flowers, is a good starting point. Some couples choose flamboyant decorations, or may even opt for a themed party, while others go for elegant understatement.

LIGHTING

The lighting in the reception venue creates the ambience, sets the tone and should be considered carefully. Bright lights are a mood-killer. Dimmers must always be used to create a romantic, flattering light, but don't go too far; too little light will also deaden the atmosphere.

Pin spots, directed at each table centre, can bring flower arrangements alive and create movement in the room. They can also be used to highlight other arrangements or focal points and features in the reception venue.

Nothing beats candlelight for a natural, romantic light. Groups of flickering tealights or candles, if allowed, will create a magical atmosphere, but avoid scented candles as they can become overpowering. If candles are banned, then fairy lights are a good alternative. These can be used to highlight entrances, arches and doorways.

Colour lighting effects can be used to boost the party spirit. They are an effective way of changing the mood after the sit-down dinner, marking a break from the formalities and the beginning of music and dancing.

In a marquee, up-lighters provide a sophisticated light inside, and make the marquee glow from the outside. If it is a summer wedding, and guests are likely to be strolling outside, a well-lit, glowing marquee will add to the festive atmosphere.

OUTSIDE

The exterior must not be forgotten if the reception is in a venue or marquee with a garden. Strings of coloured fairy lights, a few lit trees, flares or well-placed candles can extend the party ambience beyond the main room. Paths should be well lit to prevent accidents; tiki torches planted in the ground or hanging paper lanterns are two good ways of doing this.

FLOWERS

Flowers are often the main source of decoration at the reception. The bride and groom should meet the florist and talk through the theme and style of their wedding, along with budgetary constraints. Keeping it simple and not using too many different types of flowers often achieves the most sophisticated results. One easy way of

maintaining a strong theme throughout the reception venue is to use just one type of bloom, perhaps with a little greenery such as ivy. This is an economical option that will also have a strong visual impact.

Arrangements should be placed where they will be most prominent: along walkways; at the corners of the room or marquee; and on the cake table. If the venue is very large, and space needs filling, architectural plants in large urns are an option. Specialist hire companies will also be able to supply small trees and branches. These larger plants will have a dramatic impact, especially when they are lit by an uplighter or a pinspot. Flowers and greenery can be wired together to form a swag; these floral garlands can be used to frame doorways, windows and archways.

Pew-end flower arrangements from the ceremony venue should be brought to the reception and put on the back of the bridal party's chairs by an usher. So long as the vicar/officiant is agreeable, one or two of the large floral arrangements can also be transported to the reception.

Table Decorations

TABLES

Whether square, rectangular or round tables have been chosen, full sized tablecloths that come down to the floor should be used. Don't forget extra tables for the table place cards (if a seating plan display board isn't being used), bar, cake and presents. It is also useful to supply occasional tables for the drinks reception, where guests will be able to leave discarded glasses.

CHAIRS

A wide variety of chairs are available for hire at a range of prices. The cheapest are standard gold or silver banqueting chairs. There are also bamboo-like, ladder-backed chivari chairs or modern, sleek high-backed dining chairs. Fabric covers can be hired separately. They can be paired with organza ribbons in a range of colours. However, this is an expensive option and, once they have been sat on, can look messy.

TABLE SETTINGS

Crockery, linen and table centres combine to create an overall decorative effect. Details, such as menus and place cards, should be thought through carefully and fit the style of the wedding.

Table centres are crucial, and are part of the overall floral design. High and low floral arrangements on alternating tables will add interest to the room. Candelabra and tall vases are a good way of achieving the required height without obstruction. Sight lines on the tables must be kept clear; guests should be able to see everyone at the table without having to peer around large arrangements.

Unusual china or coloured glass can help add to a theme or style. Classic white linen and clear glass create a timeless, traditional effect, while coloured napkins or linen make a bold statement.

Napkin rings, or equivalent, provide a chance to introduce some detail and coordinating colour to the table. It is more effective to have an unusual napkin fastening than to have them folded in some sophisticated origami. A single flower is a popular choice.

CANDLES

Other decorations, such as tealight holders, are often available to hire from the florist. Make sure eight-hour burning candles are used, not the standard four-hour ones. It is advisable to place a drop of water in the bottom of the tealight holders when using eight-hour burners to prevent them from overheating and shattering.

PLACE AND TABLE NAMES

The table numbers or names and place cards should also fit the theme of the table decorations. They can be simple and plain, or decorative. Hand calligraphy is perfectly acceptable, and place cards can be hand-made at home, rather than printed.

Decorative Details

HATS

Space must be allocated for ladies to leave their hats. An area in the ladies' lavatory will suffice, or there may be a dedicated cloakroom.

Hats can, however, provide a form of decoration and colour. Place a spare table near the entrance to the reception upon which hats can be heaped; alternatively, hang them on ribbon with wooden or decorative pegs.

PRESENTS

Make sure there is an obvious area at the reception venue where guests can leave presents that are brought on the day. If the venue is not secure or private, then the presents should be moved to a secure area once they have all been left at the beginning of the reception. Someone,

usually a bridesmaid or usher, must be responsible for taking them away at the end of the day.

FAVOURS

Wedding favours are becoming increasingly popular. The most sophisticated favours are also expensive.

Traditionally, five sugared almonds in organza were given to the women, tied with a decorative ribbon. They represent health, happiness, fertility, wealth and long life. Sugared almonds are still a popular and cost-effective choice with many brides. There are many other options:

※ In a break with tradition, favours designed specifically for men are now available, for example bottle-stoppers, cufflinks and corkscrews.

✳ Favours are especially well received by children; sweets or something to play with are good choices.

✳ Other favours range from small trinkets to more extravagant monogrammed mementos. Popular ideas include: miniature bottles of alcohol; personalised chocolates; decorative candles; keyrings.

Ensure when choosing favours that they fit in with the overall decorative theme of the wedding. Be careful that they do not form an obstruction on the table or clash with the place settings. They can be a charming gesture, provide a point of interest and will contribute to the table decorations. They are, however, often forgotten about at the end of the day and end up being a waste of money.

Some couples request that an announcement is made at the end to remind people to take them. Costs for tasteful and worthwhile favours quickly add up. The bride and groom must work out if the cost is worth it, and what they are sacrificing elsewhere.

CAMERAS

Good-looking disposable cameras, which come in a range of colours – from gold and silver to ivory and lilac – are designed especially for weddings. They can be placed on each table, and guests are invited to take their own pictures of the big day.

However, developing costs can mount up, and disposable cameras can be a wasted expense that promises more that it delivers. Guests will frequently take repetitive pictures and forget to activate the flash, and the prints are often disappointing.

It may be a better idea to ask a few reliable friends – of different ages for variety – with a good eye to snap away instead. If the pictures are taken on digital cameras, they are very easily emailed between guests.

If disposable cameras are made available, it is a good investment to give one to every child. They will enjoy playing with their own camera, and will not monopolise a camera intended for an entire table.

Food: The Basics

Good food, excellent presentation and first-rate service are essential factors in making the day a resounding success. The best policy is to keep food simple, seasonal and of the highest quality that the budget will allow. The hosts should choose a menu that will suit a range of tastes, not just what they enjoy eating.

CHOOSING A CATERER

As always, personal recommendation is the best option. The bride and groom should talk to a number of different caterers and get a range of menus, ideas and quotes. The caterer will also be able to advise on presentation of the food, timings, table settings and so on. Local companies are the most cost effective, as travel costs for the caterer and all the staff will be charged. It is usually essential to do a tasting before booking.

EXPECTATIONS

The bride and groom must ask caterers a number of questions: When will the caterers arrive? When will the tables be laid? At what point will the staff clear away? What happens to leftovers? Will the caterers pack up on the day or come back the next morning? Will waiting staff need to be tipped? Does the quote include the hire of crockery, glassware and cutlery? Does the quote include VAT?

STAFF

It is essential that there are enough staff on the day. At the very minimum, there should be one waiter/waitress per 15 guests for sit-down catering. Many couples also check what the front of house staff will be wearing and provide alternatives, such as different coloured shirts.

THE OPTIONS

There are generally three options for the food at the reception: canapés only, a buffet, or a sit-down lunch or dinner. These vary in price and style.

It is best to choose a sit-down lunch or dinner rather than a buffet. Although it is more expensive and usually requires more staff, a greater sense of occasion and social cohesion will be achieved. Table seating plans can be manipulated to encourage mixing amongst guests, conversation flows and all the guests can eat at the same time. If budget dictates, then a buffet is the more economic option. There must be plenty of staff and an organised procedure to ensure that it runs efficiently.

ALTERNATIVES

If the regulation sit-down three courses is not to the couple's taste, then alternatives such as hot dog or fish and chip vans can be innovative talking points. There are a number of other less formal options, such as a hog roast or a barbecue table, where guests can help themselves to food buffet-style.

LATE NIGHT FOOD

If a long day of partying is planned, having some food available later on in the evening is advisable; something simple like bacon butties or kedgeree will be well received in the small hours after a night of dancing.

Cheese boards are also a good option. They can be set out on tables later in the evening, and hungry guests can help themselves.

DON'T FORGET

※ Ensure that the caterer has made extra vegetarian dishes in case any guests have forgotten to inform the host. Inform the caterer of any more specific dietary requirements (nut allergies, for example) beforehand.

※ Food should be provided for the photographer and the band or DJ.

※ Food must be provided for anyone else working on site, such as the car park attendant.

Food: Beginning to End

CANAPÉS

Canapés, although expensive, are a must. Guests may have missed breakfast or lunch in the rush to get to the ceremony and will not want to drink for over an hour on an empty stomach. Allow at least six canapés per person pre-lunch or dinner and 14 or more per person for a drinks and canapés-only reception.

A good combination is 50 per cent hot, 50 per cent cold, ensuring that at least 30 per cent are vegetarian. Only one type of canapé should be presented on each serving plate, and staff should be briefed to inform the guests what they are. Avoid messy canapés that are hard to eat, or likely to spill on to wedding finery. Crisps and nuts are a rather mundane choice; they will leave hands greasy and are best avoided.

THE STARTER

A simple starter is the most effective. A cold vegetarian option is easy as it requires fewer ovens in the kitchen or catering tent and suits every guest. The staff should bring the starters out once everyone is seated rather than have them ready on the tables.

THE MAIN COURSE

If there is a buffet, the staff should indicate when each table can go and collect their food. Ensure that plenty of people are serving and check that the caterer has allowed for meat-eaters to eat the vegetarian option.

For a sit-down lunch or dinner a dish that is ready and served on a single plate is the most sensible choice. Alternatively, meat or fish can be served on a plate, and guests can help themselves to bowls of salad and potatoes. Another option is to have a dish that one guest is nominated to serve to the rest of the table, creating interaction and conversation among the guests. Silver service requires skilled staff and is likely to make the serving of food slow cumbersome and dated.

When choosing the menu, the bride and groom must consider the time of year – shepherd's pie on a hot summer's day is not to everyone's taste, while cold food would seem unappetising for a winter wedding. They should also be aware of the age range of their guests: small children and the elderly are less likely to eat a hearty dinner than young adults, and may have more conservative tastes. Smell is another consideration; deep fat frying or dishes such as curry may overpower the venue. It is better to play it safe than to have guests leaving ambitious, fussy food.

PUDDING

The pudding should be indulgent, but not too rich, and beautifully decorated. Individual plates, served at the tables, work best. In summer heat, avoid dishes that are likely to melt and collapse between the kitchen and the table, such as ice cream.

Many modern couples choose to serve their wedding cake as pudding, accompanied by a coulis or berries. This option is discussed further in the section on wedding cakes.

COFFEE AND TEA

Trays of coffee cups and saucers that are brought to the tables and laid out by the staff often don't get used. Not everyone at the table will have coffee, so it is a waste of staff time and the table will look cluttered with unused cups and saucers.

It is cost- and time-effective to set up a separate coffee station away from the tables. Once the speeches are over, guests will get up to help themselves to coffee, and this will encourage them to circulate. Ensure that besides coffee, tea and herbal teas are also offered. Big jars of petits fours and slices of wedding cake can also be placed on the serving table, and guests can choose when to help themselves to these.

Drink

There are two golden rules: never run out of alcohol and never ask guests to pay for their drinks.

RECEPTION DRINKS

Keep it simple and serve champagne, if possible. Allow half a bottle per person. Pimms is a popular alternative in the summer. There should always be some beer and wine at the ready for those who don't like what's served.

Sparkling elderflower cordial is a good non-alcoholic option. It can be jazzed up with some fresh apple or pear juice, fresh lemon and ginger. This should be served in champagne flutes, with a piece of fruit in the bottom – such as a raspberry or frozen grapes – so that the waiting staff can easily spot who is and isn't drinking champagne when topping drinks up.

Guests should be offered a drink on arrival; several waiters must be positioned at the entrance to the reception. Service should be seamless; guests should never be left with an empty glass, unless they have refused a top-up.

THE WEDDING BREAKFAST

Serve both red and white wine, along with still and sparkling water. Allow one bottle of wine and one litre of water per person.

If the budget will allow, a sophisticated touch is to have wine waiters rather than bottles on tables. This will require one waiter for every two tables, and may stretch staff resources. Alternatively, have the wine bottles on the tables, and allow guests to top themselves up. The staff must never let a table run dry.

TOASTS

A glass of champagne should be given to each guest before the speeches; a demi-sec is a good touch if something sweet is being served after the speeches.

AFTERWARDS

A bar must be running to the very end of the reception and should be manned at all times. One barman is needed per 100 guests. Beer as well as wine should be served, and copious quantities of still and sparkling water should be available. Cocktails and spirits are a budgetary decision. In cold weather, hot toddies or mulled wine are instant warmers.

CONSIDERATIONS

✳ The supplier's returns policy must be checked; caterers should not open all bottles in advance in case they are not all needed.

✳ Hired venues may insist on supplying the wine, or charge corkage. Check corkage fees beforehand.

✳ The staff should be informed of the type of wines being served so that they are prepared if guests enquire as to what they are drinking.

Choosing the Cake

The wedding cake is a focal point of the reception, and ideally the cake will reflect the theme and colour scheme of the wedding. Cutting the cake is now a key event of the day and is considered an ideal photo opportunity.

Ensure that the cake is placed on a sturdy table that will not wobble during the cutting. After the cake has been cut, the caterers take it away, divide it up and serve it. Guests can enjoy a slice with their coffee, or later on in the evening.

CAKE-MAKERS

Each cake-maker has their own style and area of expertise; this is a highly specialised skill and standards can vary enormously.

The bride and groom should go for a tasting and discuss their wishes. They will then choose a cake from a portfolio, or order a bespoke one made to their requirements and sketched by the cake-maker.

DECORATION

✳ The cake should complement the setting. If it is competing with lavish surroundings it will need to be highly coloured or decorative.

✳ The cake must include some bold detail as it will generally be viewed from a distance.

✳ Choose a well-proportioned table, enhanced with floral decorations, that does not dwarf the cake.

TYPE

Not everyone likes fruitcake, so other options such as carrot, chocolate or lemon may be considered. A tiered cake of different flavours – for example, one chocolate tier, one lemon tier, etc. – is a good solution.

A display of cup cakes, decorated with different types of icing or flowers, or a *croquembouche* – a tall triangular pyramid of filled profiteroles drizzled with molten cascading sugar – are also good non-traditional options.

Cake Considerations

CAKE AS PUDDING

It is economical to double up the wedding cake as the pudding. Obviously, this is not a suitable option for fruitcake, and something more pudding-like must be chosen. A tower of desserts or a selection of mini-puddings stacked high is impressive and different.

If the couple still want the cake-cutting to be one of the focal points of the day, they can incorporate a small cake into the design of the pudding – for example, a sponge, served with berries or a fruit coulis.

CONSIDERATIONS

✄ Ask the cake-maker if they will be serving the cake on a silver tray or a cardboard base that needs covering.

✄ Check that the cake-maker is able to deliver to the reception venue on the day. They should have a special refrigerated van if the weather is hot.

✄ If the cake-maker is not available to assemble the cake when it is delivered, the caterer should be briefed on what it is supposed to look like and, preferably, provided with a photograph.

✄ Rather than serving the cake straight after lunch or dinner, it is often a popular option later in the evening when people are hungry again.

✄ Slices of cake should be left in a prominent position so that it is not forgotten by guests, who can help themselves during the party.

HOMEMADE

Often, a relative or friend will volunteer to make the cake. This provides a personal touch, and is certainly a cheaper option. Once the cake has been baked, however, it should be handed on to a professional to be iced, as this is a highly skilled process. Ensure that this is organised in advance and that the bride and groom aren't left with an un-iced fruit cake.

If they decide to have the whole thing made by a friend, they should think it through carefully. They may come to regret having anything that looks too home-made at the reception, where it will stand out in marked contrast to beautiful decorations and professionally laid tables.

CAKE TABLE

A separate table for the cake must be allocated. This is normally just a small round table with a white cloth.

The cake table should be dressed with fresh flowers and a knife ready beside it. If the handle is unattractive, wrap grosgrain ribbon around it.

TRADITIONS

A number of traditions are associated with the wedding cake, which is said to symbolise the couple's shared life together. Traditionally, the top tier of the fruitcake was kept back for the couple's first child's christening. It was also once believed that any single person who slept with a slice of wedding cake under their pillow would dream that night of their future spouse.

When cutting the cake, the groom should place his right hand over the bride's right hand. They make the cut together, and the bride takes the first bite, then hands the piece to the groom. Considered old fashioned by some, it is still customary to send a slice of fruitcake to those unable to attend the wedding. Other varieties of cake will not last long enough to be sent.

LEFTOVERS

With guests consuming copious quantities of drink and food, the wedding cake can easily be ignored. Ask the caterers to put leftover slices in individual cake boxes that are given to guests as they leave.

Entertainment: The Music

Music is one of the vital ingredients of the day and it is essential that it appeals to the majority of the guests, as well as enhancing the theme and style of the event. The decision must be made between a live band, or a DJ and disco.

HIRING A BAND

Personal recommendations, or a band that the couple has seen at another party, are best. Before a band is booked, it is advisable that the bride and groom see them live if at all possible. Demo CDs should not be relied upon, unless the band are booked through a reputable agency who have heard all their acts play live.

The couple must discuss with the band what type of music they want, come up with a rough playlist and check that the band is adequate to the task. They must not forget to brief the band about their chosen song for the first dance, and make sure that a range of genres and eras are covered to appeal to all the guests.

Bands will often have expectations and requests. They will require somewhere secure to store their instruments and equipment and will usually expect to eat at the same time as the guests. They will need to know precisely how long they are expected to play for, and when they will be able to take breaks. It is a good idea to have an MP3 player at the ready in case of emergency, or the party going on later than expected after the performers have gone home. Often the performers will need to be paid on the night, so the best man must have the requisite amount of cash ready and remember to attend to this.

HIRING A DJ

If the couple opt for a DJ, they should always hire a professional; asking friends, no matter how reliable, can create awkward situations if things go wrong.

Again, the bride and groom should check with the DJ that they have the first dance song and discuss their preferred playlist in advance. Many DJs provide a printed or online database, and the couple can use this to request specific songs.

EQUIPMENT AND SET UP

Whether using a live band or a DJ, it is essential to check whether the band/DJ will provide their own PA system, and what staging and lighting is required. The band or DJ should be scheduled to arrive in good time and sound check before the guests arrive.

The speakers should be set up facing into the dance floor, rather than out into the rest of the room or marquee. This will allow non-dancers to continue socialising without being drowned out by loud music.

DRINKS RECEPTION MUSIC

Jazz bands or string quartets are popular choices during the drinks reception. A live accompaniment sets a special tone for the day and creates a convivial atmosphere.

If, however, the conversation is stimulating, the champagne is flowing and the canapés circulating, then many people will not miss background music if the budget does not stretch to this.

SPECIALIST MUSIC

Countless forms of live entertainment are available. Specialist bands can be both novel and risky; the couple must be sure that they will get people involved and dancing rather than shying away from something unfamiliar.

There are many bonus extras available, but entertainment choices are usually restricted by budget. While the bride and groom should not scrimp on the entertainment aspect, it is best to invest more in one quality musical act than numerous mediocre ones.

Entertainment: Extras

If the bride and groom want to transform their reception into a memorable party, they may consider providing other forms of entertainment, which will be a talking point amongst their guests.

CASINOS

Mobile casinos provide a focal point away from the dancefloor and are thus a good option for receptions that are catering for a wide range of ages. A variety of packages will be offered, depending on the number of games required and how many guests there are. Some of the most popular options are American Roulette, Black Jack and Craps. The package will include a sufficient number of croupiers for the games being hired, who will explain the rules of the game to guests, and guide them through.

Real money is not used; the casinos provide 'fun money' and guests win prizes. A typical package provides the casino for two to three hours.

MAGICIANS

Magicians performing close-up magic can break the ice at the pre-reception drinks, or they can perform to an audience in a separate quiet area later in the evening. Another popular option is for the magician to visit the tables after guests have finished eating, when there is a slight hiatus in the proceedings before the speeches commence. Magicians will also provide an invaluable back-up solution for bored or fractious children. The couple should brief magicians clearly beforehand, giving them a precise idea of the times at which they would like them to be circulating and performing.

OTHER SUGGESTIONS

❈ For a carnival feel, stilt walkers can circulate during drinks and, later, fire eaters can perform for the guests.

❈ Chocolate fountains, with a variety of dipping fruits and other treats such as marshmallows, can be hired for the evening; an opportunity for the guests to indulge themselves after they have finished dinner.

❈ On hot summer evenings ice cream vans can provide guests with something sweet after dinner and are a popular choice with children.

❈ Mobile cocktail bars are an alternative to the expected beer and wine and become a focal show piece, with professional barmen shaking drinks in flamboyant style.

❈ Special entertainment, such as a clown or face painting, is a good idea if there are lots of children at the reception. This should take place in a separate area or kids-zone.

FIREWORKS

Fireworks are the ultimate grand finale. This is a major budgetary consideration; a considerable amount needs to be spent to make a firework display truly impressive. An announcement should be made to notify guests that the display is starting. A cheaper option, which still looks impressive, is to send the bride and groom off with sparklers. Two sparklers are distributed to each of the guests — one lit and one unlit. The unlit sparkler is a back-up in case the bride and groom are late leaving.

CONSIDERATIONS

❈ Entertainment, such as a casino or a magician, requires a quiet area away from the music.

❈ The above options will involve a substantial extra cost; think carefully before contemplating them.

❈ Make sure the entertainment doesn't irritate the guests. It should attract their attention and be of interest, rather than embarrassing or intrusive.

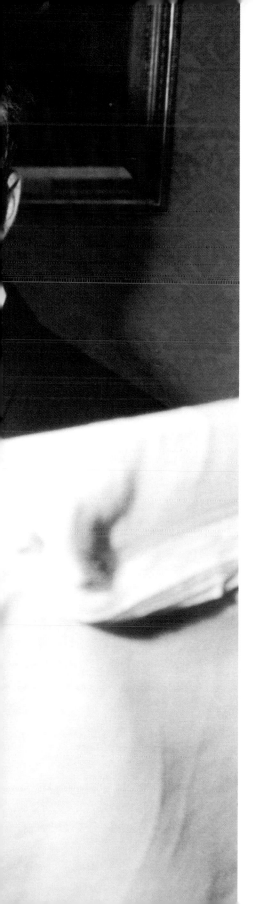

Guiding Guests

The guests must be nurtured and looked after throughout the day; bewildered and confused participants will detract from the party atmosphere. A small amount of organisation will ensure that the day runs smoothly, and every effort should be made to make each guest feel special.

INFORMATION

The wedding team should act as a point of contact. They must know exactly when the key events of the day — photographs, speeches, cake cutting, lunch or dinner, dancing and the departure of the bride and groom — are taking place. Meanwhile, the bride and groom must circulate and speak to as many of the guests as possible.

MASTER OF CEREMONIES

It is essential that someone is nominated and fully briefed to make the necessary announcements at the correct time. A professional master of ceremonies adds a flamboyant flavour to the day. He makes all the necessary announcements and ensures that guests are in the right place at the right time. Generally, a flat fee is charged for the whole day.

If the couple want a more informal approach, the chief usher or an extrovert male friend who enjoys performing in public and perhaps didn't make it as an usher is a good alternative.

CONSIDERATIONS

❋ Keep the guests happy and well informed, with good signage at the reception venue and clear announcements. Ensure that all members of the wedding team are giving out consistent information.

❋ Tell guests in advance when the bride and groom are planning on leaving and, if it's early, whether the party will carry on afterwards.

Organising Guests

TRANSPORT

In some cases, transport will have been laid on for the guests in the form of a minibus or coach. The guests will already have been informed of this in the information pack sent out with the invitations. It is essential, however, that the master of ceremonies makes an announcement to remind them of details and timings.

If guests are sorting out their own transport arrangements, local taxi firms should be warned in advance of the approximate time that there may be a demand for cars. They may be able to draft in extra drivers to cope with the large numbers, and this will prevent the problem of tired guests waiting about aimlessly. Ensure that the best man and ushers have plenty of taxi numbers to hand, or that numbers are displayed in a prominent place. This is less of a problem at city weddings where taxis may be hailed off the street.

ACCOMMODATION

The host – usually the mother of the bride – should check that guests have somewhere to stay. Often, a recommended list of suitable places is supplied with the invitation.

In some cases, especially during busy summer months, it is a good idea for the hosts to block-book local hotels and B&Bs to secure rooms. An early block-booking may also secure a significant discount. Guests can then phone up and change the booking into their name.

If a block-booking is made, an early check-in should be organised. Often, hotels and B&Bs will have a mid-afternoon check-in time, which will be too late for wedding guests who want to check into their rooms and get ready before they have to leave for the ceremony. If this is not possible, a secure area for guests to leave their luggage can be arranged. Warn hotels and B&Bs that groups of guests may be arriving late in the evening.

If the reception is taking place in a hotel, it is often possible to book all of the hotel's guest rooms at a favourable rate.

PARKING

Parking should be organised beforehand and guests should be advised as to where to park. The elderly, disabled and those who are not staying for the evening must be given priority access.

It is advisable to employ a parking attendant for security reasons and to make sure the available space is best used. The parking area, and access to and from it, should be floodlit.

If the parking area is on grass, and the ground is uneven, vehicle tracking to prevent tyres sinking may be needed; this can be costly and is charged by the metre.

THE BIG DAY

The Night Before

The night before the wedding should be an oasis of calm before the exhilaration of the big day. It is recommended that the bride and groom follow tradition and do not spend the evening before the wedding together if at all possible, for both customary and practical reasons. The excitement of seeing each other the next day will be intensified, while working each other up into a nervous frenzy is not wise.

During the day or early evening there will probably have been a ceremony rehearsal, where all the final logistics, timings and expectations will have been run through and all the wedding party carefully briefed. By the evening, everything should be in the capable hands of the best man or chief usher; last-minute panic should be unnecessary as everybody involved will know what is expected of them the following day.

It is essential for the couple to snatch a few moments together before going their separate ways, knowing that the next time they see each other will be on their wedding day. They can offer mutual encouragement, and remind each other why they've come this far. The evening is an opportunity for the bride and groom to relax and spend time reminiscing with parents or close friends. It goes without saying that getting drunk, or even tipsy, is a bad idea. An early night is advisable; if sleep is impossible, the bride and groom should at least try to rest and relax.

It is best to keep the evening as low-key as possible and save everyone's energy for the wedding. A small dinner for close family only is a good way to spend the evening before the wedding; a larger pre-wedding dinner should be held two nights in advance, if possible, to keep stress levels to a minimum.

DINNERS

Pre-wedding dinners for family and close friends are an ideal time to get together and discuss the approaching day. They can be held in a hotel or restaurant, or in the more informal atmosphere of the parents' home. They are a good way for the bride (and groom) to spend time with any relatives or friends who have travelled long distances to attend the wedding and who otherwise may only be seen briefly on the big day.

TIME OUT?

The couple should talk through the pros and cons of whether it's a good idea to spend some time apart in the final run-up to the wedding. A bit of space will encourage calmness and reflection, much needed at this point in a bride or groom's schedule. Nevertheless, it is a good idea for the couple to speak to each other every day, voice hopes, expectations and fears, and discuss how the plans are going for the day itself.

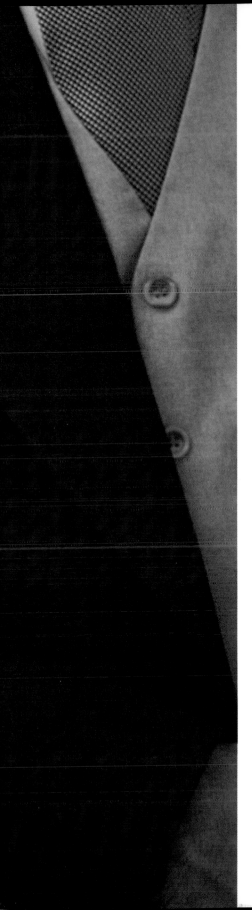

Schedule of the Day

The bride and groom should plan out the events of the day so they can make the best use of the time, and inform their suppliers of an expected running order. Ensure that time is allowed for getting from the ceremony venue to the reception, if applicable.

The following is a rough guideline:

CHURCH OR CIVIL CEREMONY
20–60 minutes.

PHOTOGRAPHS AFTER THE CEREMONY
15 minutes (including 5 minutes for pictures of the bride and groom, 10 minutes for other shots).

DRINKS RECEPTION
90 minutes, usually extends to 2 hours (a receiving line takes about 40 minutes and well organised photographs take 20–30 minutes).

SEATING GUESTS
Up to 30 minutes.

THE WEDDING BREAKFAST
2 hours for three courses.

SPEECHES
30 minutes, usually extending to 45 minutes (at least 10 minutes per person, assuming there are three speakers).

CAKE CUTTING
15–30 minutes.

DANCING
Approximately three hours (depending upon when the bride and groom leave, and how long the party lasts).

GOING AWAY
15 minutes (throwing bouquet and saying goodbye).

The Morning

Traditionally, the bride and groom spend the night before the wedding apart. If they decide not to, then they should set off early on the day of the wedding to the place where they will each be getting ready.

The bridesmaids, best man and ushers must be at the bride and groom's respective locations in plenty of time if they have not been there the night before. It is best only to have the key players around at this stage; too many people milling about makes it difficult for everyone to get ready.

Never underestimate how much there is to do, no matter how much has been organised beforehand. It is always sensible to allow extra contingency time for last-minute crises and delays.

THE BRIDE

All eyes will be on the bride, and she is the main priority; plenty of time must be allocated to get her ready. Rushing causes fraught nerves and accidents.

 No matter how nervous she is the bride should try to eat something.

She should put on her underwear before she has her hair and make-up done.

Once the bride's hair and make-up is ready, the chief bridesmaid and mother of the bride should be the next to prepare, followed by any remaining bridesmaids. This gives the chief bridesmaid and mother of the bride time to help the bride into her dress.

※ The bride should put her dress on, followed by the shoes and veil or headdress, half an hour before leaving. Jewellery should be added last of all.

※ If the wedding dress goes on over her head, make sure her face is fully covered with a scarf so as not to ruin either her make-up or the dress.

※ Anyone helping the bride should wear clean white gloves and no shoes.

※ Plenty of time should be allowed to get the bride into her dress, which is likely to have complicated fastenings. Although there should have been a practice run, nervous fumbling is inevitable.

※ Once dressed, the bride should avoid sitting down to avoid creasing the back of the dress.

※ She should take a few moments to compose herself and enjoy a glass of champagne with her parents and bridesmaids.

THE GROOM AND BEST MAN

While getting dressed is a less drawn-out procedure for the men, they should still allow plenty of time to avoid unnecessary panic.

※ It is traditional for the groom, best man and ushers to meet for breakfast or lunch before going to the church or ceremony venue.

※ They should double-check that all the components of their suits are ready, and that they have all the necessary accessories, such as cufflinks and tie-pins.

※ The best man and groom should have a final run-through of their speeches (separately) if required.

※ The best man should reconfirm that all the cars and taxis will arrive on time and know where they are going.

※ The best man should check on buttonholes and rings and gather any cards, emails or telemessages that are to be read out at the reception.

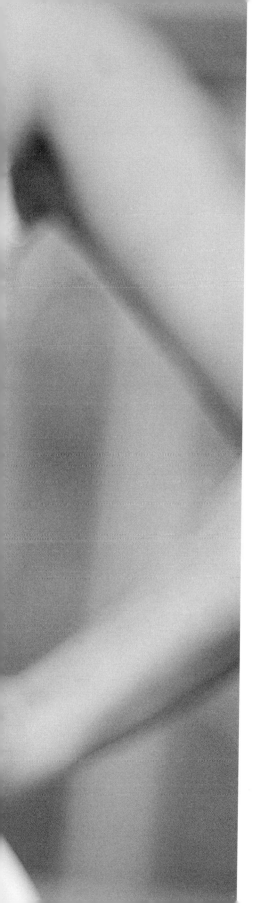

Practicalities

There are various items that the groom, best man and chief bridesmaid need to remember to take with them on the big day.

CHIEF BRIDESMAID

The chief bridesmaid should carry everything the bride will need on the day, including make-up for touch ups, in a small, elegant handbag.

She should also have a mobile phone so that she can contact the best man if necessary, or be the point of contact for the bridal party.

If required, the bride's overnight bag, handbag and other essentials for the following day can be left at the reception venue in advance.

The bridesmaids should also leave everything they might need at the reception venue, such as a change of shoes (pumps, flip-flops), camera and a wrap or shawl.

THE GROOM

The groom will need a mobile phone and his speech notes. Presents for the bridesmaids, car keys (if needed), cash and an overnight bag can all be left at the reception venue the day before.

He can also arrange for flowers for the mothers to be delivered to the reception venue that morning.

THE BEST MAN

The best man will need the rings, his mobile phone, speech notes, spare cash and enough money to cover church fees and final payments for the relevant suppliers.

He must have a note of all emergency transport or contact numbers (including the chief bridesmaid's and caterer's phone numbers). It is a good idea to bring a fountain pen for signing the register.

175

Arrival and Duties

CEREMONY ARRIVAL TIMES

It is important that everybody involved arrives at the ceremony venue in good time. There is a fine line between arriving too early and nervously waiting around and having to rush to be there on time. Here are some suggested timings:

Ushers: 45 minutes before.

Best man and groom: 45–30 minutes before.

Guests: up to 30 minutes before.

Groom's parents: 15 minutes before.

Mother of bride and bridesmaids: 10 minutes before.

Bride and father: 5 minutes before.

USHERS' DUTIES

The ushers will be the first to arrive at the church/ register office and will have several key tasks.

Distributing the orders of service, including leaving some at the front for the wedding party. Ensuring that the officiant has the order of service for the bride and groom.

Casting an eye over the flowers to make sure they are placed as the bride and groom intended.

Checking whether there is a PA system in the church for readings and, if not, letting the readers know in advance that they may have to speak up.

Checking the reserved seating. Usually a few rows at the front are reserved for immediate family members and the wedding party, but there may also be special seating for elderly or disabled guests. If there are couples with very young children it may be a good idea to ensure that seats next to the aisle are allocated to them.

If there are lavatories at the ceremony venue, checking that they work and are fully equipped.

One or two ushers should be briefed to supervise the parking and ensure easy access for the bridal cars. A space should also be reserved for the photographer.

Distributing buttonholes to the groom, best man and ushers. Checking that the father of the groom also has a buttonhole.

Ensuring that any soloists or musicians know their cues and where they should stand.

If it's a hot day, making sure there are bottles of water on standby.

Last Moments

The final hour before the ceremony is likely to be a tense and nervous time. After months of planning the big day is irrevocably underway and the sense of anticipation mounting.

THE GROOM AND BEST MAN
The groom and best man arrive shortly after the ushers. Provided the ushers were well briefed and have fulfilled their duties, they will arrive to an atmosphere of organised calm. The best man should make final checks.

THE BRIDAL PARTY
If the ceremony is taking place in a busy location and traffic is a concern, then provision should be made. Both bridal cars should arrive for their pick ups in plenty of time, and if necessary circle the area near the ceremony venue until the appointed arrival time.

The mother of the bride and the bridesmaids leave for the ceremony first; they should aim to arrive ten minutes before it is due to start.

The mother of the bride is the last person to be seated; a selected usher should accompany her to her seat.

The bridesmaids will wait at the entrance of the building for the bride to arrive.

The bride and her father – or whoever is giving her away or accompanying her to the church or ceremony venue – will be left alone for a few final moments. These are likely to be memorably emotional and highly-charged.

By the time the bride arrives, the groom, best man and guests should be in their places. The ushers will be overseeing any final arrivals and checks.

The bridal party should take a few moments to compose themselves, arrange veils, trains, bouquets and so on.

LATECOMERS
If guests arrive late, they wait until the bride has completed her walk up the aisle before entering.

Ceremony Highlights

Every wedding has highlights that will stay in the memory. The entire congregation will be looking forward to these moments.

THE ENTRANCE OF THE BRIDE

This is the dramatic opening of proceedings; guests may have been waiting some time for the bride's arrival and the sense of expectation is high. Before the bride begins to proceed up the aisle, she must allow the chief bridesmaid to make final checks and arrange her dress, train and veil.

The officiant waits for the bride at the entrance to the ceremony venue (for example the church door). The bridal party take up their positions, which will have been rehearsed beforehand. It is usual for the chief bridesmaid to walk directly behind the bride, followed by the other bridesmaids. If there are baby bridesmaids or pageboys it may be a good idea for the adult bridesmaids to take their hands and guide them up the aisle.

The bride takes the right arm of her father (or the person giving her away). The officiant signals for the organist or musicians to start and the opening music begins. This is the cue for the groom and best man that the bride has entered the building, and for the bride and her father to start walking.

The pace should have been agreed upon and practised by the whole procession; nerves will naturally speed people up, but it is best to go slowly as all of the guests will want to look at the bride. The bride should remember to hold herself upright with her shoulders back.

Once she reaches the groom and best man at the front, the officiant will begin the service. It is usual for the bride's veil to be taken back (by her mother or the chief bridesmaid) and her bouquet is given to the chief bridesmaid during the first hymn.

VOWS

The vows should be said clearly and confidently, as previously rehearsed with the officiant. The moment will pass quickly, so the couple should concentrate and enjoy saying them.

If any names are muddled up or lines forgotten, a sense of humour helps and the officiant will step in to rectify the situation.

THE FIRST KISS

A first kiss, if there is one, follows the vows. The kiss should be rehearsed to strike the right balance between respect and passion; a round of applause may follow. This is a key moment of the day for the bride and groom.

RECESSIONAL

The bride and groom walk back down the aisle, followed by the wedding party. There is generally an atmosphere of great happiness and relief; the serious part of the day is now over, the celebrations are about to begin and the couple are officially Mr and Mrs.

The Party Begins

After the photographs have been taken outside the ceremony venue, everyone makes their way to the reception. The ease and timing of this depends upon the location of the reception. If the reception is in a separate venue, the ushers should now come into their own, organising both guests and transport.

Once the bride, groom and wedding party have left, the ushers can tactfully direct any loitering guests towards their cars or onto transport heading for the reception. They should be aware of the projected timings of the day, and move people on to avoid delays. Either the best man or chief bridesmaid should take responsibility for phoning the caterers to let them know that the bride and groom have left the ceremony venue. There is nothing worse than arriving at an unprepared reception.

A couple of ushers must stay behind and clear up the venue – gathering order of service sheets, checking for belongings left behind – before heading to the reception. They can also collect pew-end flower arrangements for the reception, if applicable.

RECEIVING LINES

Receiving lines are a chance for the hosts to greet everybody arriving at the wedding reception. They are necessary for large or very formal weddings, or when the reception is very short – for example champagne and canapés for only a couple of hours. They provide an opportunity for the bride and groom to speak to and meet all the guests, but an average receiving line will take up to 45 minutes of the reception drinks time, which can put some couples (and guests) off the idea.

Many couples decide to have a receiving line no matter how many guests they have present or how long the reception. It is an entirely personal choice.

If there is a receiving line, the ushers must point guests in the right direction. The caterers must be briefed to give guests a drink while they are waiting, and provide top-ups if the line is slow.

Traditionally, both sets of parents, the bride and groom, the best man and the chief bridesmaid receive the guests. Alternatively, a receiving line can consist of just the bride, groom and both sets of parents.

It is advisable for the wedding party to stand opposite each other or in an informal group, rather than in an actual line. This ensures that people keep moving along and that guests can be introduced with ease. It encourages natural conversation and avoids the stiff formality of guests having to repeat their name to each member of the wedding party as they move along the receiving line.

If the couple choose to receive the guests on their own, proceedings can be kept brief and informal. The parents, best man and chief bridesmaid can circulate freely and introduce guests to each other.

If there is no receiving line at all, then the couple must visit every table at the reception.

RECEPTION DRINKS

There should be a clear area for drinks once guests arrive at the reception. If it is in a large open space, guests should be gathered into one area to maintain atmosphere.

If guests are standing on grass, a canopy or gazebo with matting is a convenient sun (or rain) shield. The matting will prevent stilettos from sinking into the grass.

The beginning of the reception is a crucial time and sets the tone for the day. There must be plenty of drinks available, and the ushers should ensure that no one is feeling left out, making introductions if guests are looking isolated.

Toasts and Speeches

Toasts and speeches are both a formality, dictated by convention, and a highlight of the day – a time when everybody comes together.

There is no set rule about when the speeches should be made, and it is important that the bride and groom think through the structure of the whole reception before deciding on their exact timing. Some opt to have them early on, before eating, especially if the speakers are nervous; others adhere to tradition and have them after pudding. If it is a drinks reception, then timing is crucial – after an hour and a half is normally about right.

An excellent compromise for a seated reception is to have the speeches after the main course, but before the pudding. A glass of champagne for the toasts – a sweet one to complement the pudding is a good touch – can be circulated once the plates have been cleared.

Some couples opt to cut the cake before the speeches to prevent this part of the day from being overshadowed by the aftermath of the speeches.

The caterers should be briefed to serve the speech-makers' drinks last. They will then be able to begin their speeches confident in the knowledge that all the guests are ready, with fully charged glasses. Traditionally, the speeches begin with the father of the bride, followed by the groom and finally the best man.

CONSIDERATIONS

✳ Traditions are changing, and many brides like to add a few words themselves; this normally happens after the groom's speech.

✳ It is not uncommon for the chief bridesmaid also to say something.

✳ In a large venue, the speeches should be made with a microphone – preferably a roaming one – that has been sound checked before the guests arrive.

✳ The photographer should be briefed in advance and then signalled by the best man when the speeches are about to begin.

✳ An usher should notify any guests not in the vicinity of the speeches – for example, people outside smoking – that the speeches are about to take place.

✳ It is perfectly acceptable for speakers to refer to brief notes, so long as they do not read the entire speech directly off the page.

✳ If the bride and groom are of different nationalities, it is a good idea to provide a screen with a translation so that all the guests feel included.

Speeches: The Big Three

Traditionally, there are three speeches, delivered in a specific order with certain formalities:

⁕ Father of the bride.

⁕ The groom.

⁕ The best man.

FATHER OF THE BRIDE

He thanks the guests for coming and those involved with organising and paying for the wedding (no reference to money should ever be made). He may then indulge in some affectionate anecdotes about the bride, before welcoming the groom into the family. He finishes with a toast to 'the bride and groom'. This role can be filled by whoever gave the bride away, be it a brother or uncle.

THE GROOM

First the groom must thank the father of the bride (or equivalent) on behalf of himself and his new wife for the speech – the reference to his 'wife' usually raises a cheer from the crowd.

He must then thank the guests for coming, the bride's parents (if they are hosting the wedding), his parents for raising him and the best man for supporting him. He can also present both mothers (if applicable) with bouquets. He then says a few words about his beautiful new wife. The groom should finish his speech with a toast to 'the bridesmaids'.

THE BEST MAN

The best man's speech is expected to be the highlight of the proceedings, a witty and entertaining account of the groom, and a sincere reflection on their friendship. He should begin by reading out messages – originally telegrams and letters, nowadays usually emails and letters – from friends and relatives who couldn't attend.

He then tells a selection of stories and anecdotes about the groom. He is expected to reveal something lighthearted and fun that will embarrass the groom. The speech should also include some stories about the couple, how they met, their relationship and a few compliments for the bride.

The best man's speech should be amusing rather than shocking and must appeal to all generations. The tone should be witty, never smutty.

He finishes with a toast to 'Mr and Mrs [newly-weds' surname]'. He will then announce the cutting of the cake, if applicable.

CONSIDERATIONS

⁕ Preparation is vital. The more time is spent thinking about the speech and practising delivering it, maybe in front of a friend or partner, the more polished it will be. Only very confident speechmakers should risk ad-libbing on the day.

⁕ Speechmakers should be aware of their upcoming responsibilities, and ensure that they don't drink too much beforehand.

⁕ It is a real *faux pas* to forget to thank anyone who helped to make the day possible, get their name wrong, or mispronounce it. Pre-wedding research is essential to ensure that this does not happen.

⁕ Keep an eye on the time. Rambling reminiscences will become tedious and challenge the audience's attention span. Make sure everything that is said is relevant to the bride and groom.

⁕ Neither the father of the bride nor the best man should upstage the bride and groom – it is their day.

The First Dance

The first dance is often considered to be one of the romantic highlights of the day. The bride and groom are sharing a private moment, but the first dance is also a very public display and can be quite daunting for both; it is not common to dance together in front of a captive audience, albeit a partisan one.

The bride and groom should choose a song that suits their taste and, if they wish, keep it secret to surprise their guests. They must consider the pace and the length of the song, and check that the lyrics are appropriate for the day. While a slow love song might seem the most obvious choice, a more upbeat and fun number is perfectly acceptable – the first dance is, after all, a form of entertainment for the guests as well as being a special moment for the couple.

Professional lessons beforehand – where a teacher will choreograph a routine for the couple – are an option. They can produce a slick result, but often just a little practice will result in something memorable and natural.

The band or DJ must be briefed on when the couple will take to the floor, and must begin at exactly the right moment. The photographer must also be in place.

As the song ends, and the next track begins, the wedding party joins the couple on the dance floor to dance with each other. The groom should dance with each of the mothers, the bride with both fathers, the mother of the bride with the father of the groom, the father of the bride with the mother of the groom and the best man with the chief bridesmaid.

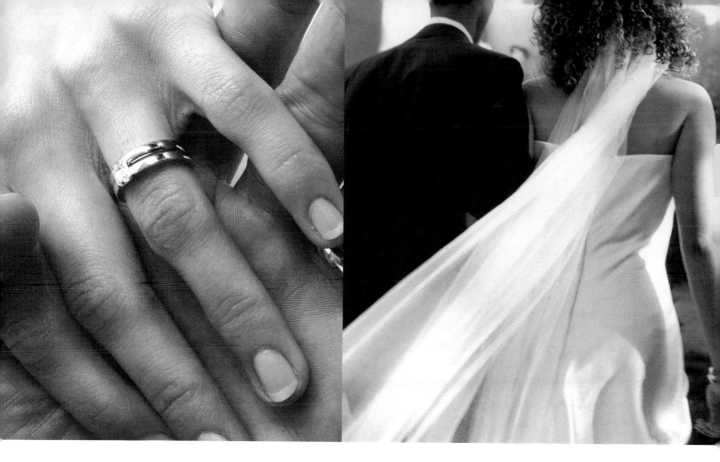

Perfect Hosts

The bride and groom are the centre of attention for the entire day. While it is important that they have a fun and memorable day, they must also ensure that they are good hosts, giving their guests a day to remember.

The couple must circulate, especially if there is no receiving line, and should not allow themselves to be monopolised by close friends and family. They should visit the tables between courses, exchanging greetings and a few words with all the guests. They must be especially aware of guests they do not know so well, or those who have travelled a long way or come from abroad. As the reception progresses and everyone relaxes, there are plenty of more informal opportunities to catch up with most guests. The bride or groom should accept every invitation to dance.

The parents, chief bridesmaid and best man should also act as hosts and aim to keep an eye out for guests attending on their own, or those who do not know many people. They must try to include them, especially when the bride and groom are circulating elsewhere.

The bride and groom can also try to spend some time alone. The best time for this is at the very beginning of the reception, while the guests are arriving. The caterer can be briefed to bring a selection of canapés and drinks for the newly-weds to an appointed quiet place or room away from the main party. The couple can then have ten minutes alone, in which to reflect on the ceremony, take in their surroundings and have a calm chat. This may be the only chance they will have to be alone together or to talk all day.

Going Away

This is the finale of the day. Many couples choose a grand departure, accompanied by fireworks, sparklers, flares or even a band. Others just drive off to a waving, cheering crowd. Arrangements are a matter of personal choice, and budget dependent.

The couple should agree on their departure time well in advance, and inform the wedding party of this. The band or DJ must also be warned that there may be a break in proceedings if they are carrying on after the couple leave.

The vehicle, usually chosen by the groom, should arrive early (so that any luggage can be transferred into it). Traditionally, the best man and ushers decorate the vehicle, but this can be impractical if, for example, it is a taxi and not personally owned.

The best man must keep a lookout for the vehicle's arrival and give the bride and groom a half-hour warning so that they can go and change if necessary. Many brides choose to wear a special going-away outfit; others decide to wear their dress to the very end. If the bride is changing, the mother of the bride or chief bridesmaid is normally asked to be on hand to help the bride get out of her dress and into her new outfit.

The best man, chief bridesmaid and family should inform the guests and the photographer of the couple's imminent departure, or ask the band or DJ to make an announcement. Everyone gathers round to scatter more confetti and watch the throwing of the bouquet.

GOODBYES

Traditionally, the throwing of the bouquet is the last thing to be done before the couple leave the reception. If the bride wishes to keep her bouquet, it is a good idea to have a spare one made up to be thrown. The single girls gather round, the bride turns her back and throws the bouquet over her head.

The couple must say personal goodbyes to those who have played a special part in the wedding. Immediate family, the best man, chief bridesmaid and close friends should be individually thanked. Once they have driven off, the guests are free to resume the celebrations.

Timing is all-important. The bride and groom do not want to be the last ones standing and leave when the party is winding down, as this will be an anticlimax. Equally, they should not leave too early and miss out on the best party they may ever have. An early departure will also upset those who have come a long way, or gone to great trouble to attend the wedding.

It is a good idea to give the guests an idea beforehand of when the bride and groom are planning to leave. The elderly or those with young children may need to make an earlier exit if the couple intend to stay until the end of the night, or they might plan to leave as soon as the bride and groom have departed.

AFTERWARDS

The Wedding Night

The bride and groom should spend their wedding night somewhere special, romantic and not too far from the reception.

If the reception is in a hotel, the couple must decide whether to stay at the venue or go somewhere else – they may want time away from other guests and family. Either way, the evening should be a unique and memorable time together as husband and wife and a quiet refuge after the whirlwind of the wedding day.

Most couples arrive high on adrenaline from the day, and desperate to talk over their experiences. Often, they will be hungry and in need of a celebratory drink alone together. Many couples make the mistake of spending a fortune on vintage champagne from room service, only to drink one glass and leave the rest. There will be so many other things on their minds – it is best to save the expense for a calmer time on honeymoon.

PRACTICALITIES

※ The hotel should be warned that the couple are newly-weds – many places give them special treatment – and whether they will be arriving late.

※ Their luggage, if possible, should have been delivered.

※ Someone, normally the best man or chief bridesmaid, should arrange for champagne and perhaps flowers to be put in the room.

※ If flying early the next day, the proximity of the hotel to the airport should be considered.

※ If the bride and groom chose not to change before they left the reception, arrangements must be made for an usher or member of the wedding party to collect their wedding clothes the following day.

Honeymoon: Practicalities

Traditionally organised by the groom and kept secret, honeymoons are now far more likely to be organised by the couple together.

RESEARCH
The trip should be researched carefully to avoid disappointment or any potentially embarrassing overlaps with previous holidays (in particular, those with previous partners). To avoid this, many couples choose to visit somewhere neither party has been to before.

CHOICE OF TRIP
It is important to choose a destination that meets the requirements of both the bride and groom. They should decide what they want from this unique and romantic time away: complete relaxation, action, adventure, culture or a combination of the above. The desired climate, accommodation, length of flights, food and activities on offer should also be taken into account.

Travel agents will talk through all the options and create bespoke trips accordingly. The bride will appreciate a surprise or two, so clever grooms will keep several aspects of the trip a secret.

TIMINGS
The time of year and budget will dictate suitable locations as well as the length of time spent on honeymoon. Most couples now spend two to three weeks away, though some seize the opportunity of time away from home and use the honeymoon as a launch pad for extended travels around the world.

SCHEDULE

When choosing the destination, couples should bear in mind that after the pressurised build-up to a wedding, a 5 a.m. start before a 13-hour flight, followed by two internal flights and a taxi ride can make tempers fray.

Comfort, luxury and privacy are essential requirements for the initial part of the honeymoon, as the couple are likely to be exhausted. The days of leaping onto a flight immediately after the wedding are long gone.

Couples should allow themselves some time to enjoy the first few days and nights of married life. Many choose to unwind in a hotel or at home (there may even be a post-wedding lunch) before jetting off.

The couple should pack well in advance: they are unlikely to have the time to do this properly during the hectic build-up to the wedding.

Note: the bride's tickets and passport must be in the same name (either maiden or married).

The groom should take responsibility for:

✳ Taxis and transfers

✳ Tickets and reservations

✳ Online check-in (being put in separate aisles of an aeroplane on honeymoon is extremely disappointing)

✳ Travel insurance

✳ Inoculations

✳ Marriage certificates

✳ Visas and passports

The newly-weds should let airlines and hotels know that they are on honeymoon: there may be the chance of upgrades, special dispensations and treats. If the couple are seeking romantic solitude, let tour operators know; they can help to make the trip special.

Honeymoon Destinations

JANUARY

✖ HOT

Mexico, Belize, Costa Rica, Caribbean, South Africa, Oman, Maldives, Thailand, Laos, Cambodia, Malaysia, Australia, New Zealand.

✖ COLD

USA (Vale), Canada (Whistler), Antarctica, Russia.

✖ SPECIAL

Barbados Jazz Festival, Caribbean; Chinese New Year, China; Ippan Sanga (Imperial Palace Entry), Tokyo, Japan; Sydney Festival, Australia.

✖ AVOID

Seychelles, Mauritius (cyclones/rainy season), Bali (rainstorms).

FEBRUARY

✖ HOT

Galapagos Islands, Belize, Costa Rica, Caribbean, South Africa, Egypt, Oman, Maldives, India (Rajasthan, Goa), Thailand, Malaysia, Australia, New Zealand.

✖ COLD

Switzerland (St Moritz, Zermatt), Antarctica, Russia.

✖ SPECIAL

Whale Watching, Baja California, Mexico; Rio de Janeiro Carnival, Brazil; Venice Carnival, Italy; Desert Festival, Jaisalmer, India; Abu Simbel Festival, Egypt; Chinese New Year, China.

✖ AVOID

Seychelles, Mauritius (cyclones/rainy season), Bali (rainstorms).

MARCH

✖ HOT

Galapagos Islands, Belize, Costa Rica, Caribbean, Namibia, Egypt, Oman, India (Goa), Malaysia.

✖ COLD

Switzerland (St Moritz, Zermatt), Russia.

✖ SPECIAL

Holi Festival, throughout India.

✖ AVOID

Seychelles, Mauritius (cyclones/rainy season), Bali (rainstorms).

APRIL

HOT

Caribbean, Belize, Costa Rica, Brazil, Morocco, Namibia, Seychelles, Mauritius, Thailand, Indonesia, Borneo, Oman, French Polynesia (Tahiti).

SPECIAL

Songkran Festival, Thailand; Easter parades in Greece, Italy, Spain and Guatemala.

AVOID

Mauritius, Eastern Africa.

MAY

HOT

Mexico, Spain, Italy, Crete, Cyprus, Turkey, Morocco, Botswana, Zambia, China (Tibet), Bhutan, Bali.

SPECIAL

Vienna Festival, Austria.

AVOID

India (extreme heat), Eastern Africa (rain).

JUNE

HOT

Bermuda, Canada, France, Portugal, Spain, Norway, Italy, Greece, Turkey, Cyprus, Botswana, Zambia, Malawi, Bali.

SPECIAL

Inti Raymi Festival of the Sun, Cusco, Peru; White Nights Festival, St Petersburg, Russia.

AVOID

Indian plains, Egypt (hot), Caribbean (cyclones/rainy season), Thailand, Maldives (rainy season).

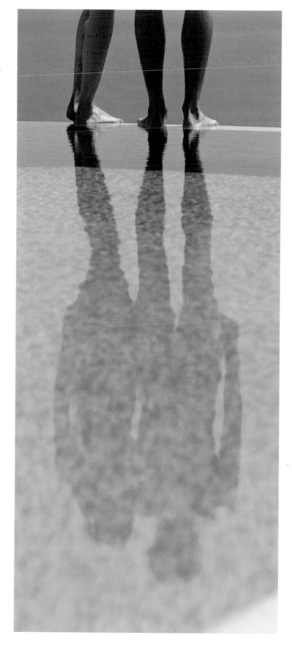

Honeymoon Destinations

JULY

HOT
Canada, Europe, Namibia, Botswana, Zambia, Kenya, China (Tibet), Malaysia (east coast), Indonesia.

COLD
New Zealand.

SPECIAL
Kandy Esala Perahera, Sri Lanka; San Fermin Festival of Pamplona (including running of the bulls), Spain; Yushu Horse Festival, Qinghai, China.

AVOID
Maldives, Thailand and Indian plains (monsoon), Mexico, Caribbean (cyclones/rainy season).

AUGUST

HOT
Europe, Indonesia, French Polynesia.

COLD
New Zealand.

SPECIAL
Puccini Opera Festival, Italy; Edinburgh International Festival, Scotland; La Tomatina, Valencia, Spain.

AVOID
Maldives, Thailand (monsoon), Caribbean (cyclones).

SEPTEMBER

HOT
Europe, Seychelles, Mauritius, Maldives, Morocco, Indonesia, Brazil.

SPECIAL
Hermanus Whale Festival, South Africa; Fall in New England, USA.

AVOID
India, Thailand (monsoon), Caribbean (cyclones).

OCTOBER

HOT
Mexico, Argentina, Chile, Brazil, Morocco, Seychelles.

SPECIAL
Abu Simbel Festival, Egypt. Festival Kreol, Seychelles; Diwali, throughout India (check local calendars).

AVOID
Thailand (monsoon).

NOVEMBER

❋ HOT
Mexico, Argentina, Chile, Brazil, Costa Rica, Belize, South Africa, Seychelles, Mauritius, Thailand.

❋ SPECIAL
Day of the Dead, Mexico; Le Salon du Chocolat, Paris, France; Berlin Jazz Festival, Germany; Pushkar Camel Fair, Rajasthan, India; Diwali, throughout India (check local calendars); Loy Krathang Festival of Light, Thailand.

❋ AVOID
Malaysia (rain), Caribbean (cyclones).

DECEMBER

❋ HOT
Mexico, Cuba, Brazil, Costa Rica, Belize, USA (Florida Keys), Zanzibar, South Africa, Oman, Vietnam, Laos, Cambodia, Mauritius, Seychelles, Thailand, Australia, New Zealand.

❋ COLD
USA (Vale), Canada (Whistler), Switzerland (St Moritz), Antarctica, Russia.

❋ SPECIAL
Weinachtsmarkts, Germany; New Year's Party, St Petersburg, Russia; Windhoek Carnival, Namibia.

❋ AVOID
Bermuda (cold), Seychelles (rainy).

KEEP A RECORD
The honeymoon will be one of the most memorable holidays a couple will ever have; take plenty of photographs and keep memorabilia, such as tickets, menus and leaflets, to reminisce over in years to come.

Coming Home and Thank Yous

Reverting to normal life after a wedding and honeymoon can be difficult. The couple will have to adjust to life without a big event to plan and deal with no longer being the centre of attention. Getting back into the swing of everyday life and responsibilities can come as quite a shock after indulging in each other's company, luxuries and extravagant expenditure.

Catching up with friends and family for an enjoyable post mortem of the wedding day and the honeymoon, choosing wedding photographs and unpacking the wedding presents can all help to ease the couple back into reality. It is a good idea for them to plan social events (perhaps involving the best man and bridesmaids) or have something to look forward to, such as a weekend away a few months after the wedding.

PRESENTS

As soon as the couple are back they should contact the wedding list company, shop or specialist to arrange a convenient delivery time for the wedding presents.

PHOTOGRAPHS

The wedding photographs should now be ready for collection (this also applies to the DVD, if one has been made). The couple need to decide which images to order.

They should then pass the album on to parents and family members so that they can place their orders. It is a good idea to check whether the bridesmaids, best man or other wedding party members want to order any prints. It usually takes around two to three weeks for prints to be delivered.

THANK YOUS

It is essential to write thank you letters as soon as possible; this should certainly be done before the weeks slip into months.

A letter from the bride and groom should acknowledge every present received. To prevent thank you letters from becoming a chore, couples should split the task.

The couple must also thank the key people who made the day possible. This should include the parents, best man and bridesmaids, and can also include everyone from the minister to the soloist, the dressmaker, the florist, the caterer and the hairdresser.

If a couple wish to use stationery that matches the wedding stationery for their thank you correspondence, they should have this printed at the same time as everything else. Although it is a nice touch, this is a luxury rather than a necessity. Some newly-weds like to enclose a photograph of the guest they are writing to, or of themselves, taken on the wedding day.

OTHER THINGS TO REMEMBER

※ It is a good idea to keep a wedding file containing notes, correspondence and photographs. This will be great to look back on in years to come and is also a good way of keeping track of what presents were received, and so on.

※ The couple should check that all paperwork and invoices are now settled with suppliers.

※ The wedding dress and morning suit should be cleaned as soon as possible to prevent any deterioration or damage that may be caused by neglect.

※ The couple will also need to collect any clothes or possessions they left with members of the family or at friends' houses before the wedding.

※ The bride can investigate companies who will pack her dress away professionally for storing, and others who will preserve her bouquet.

New Names

It is traditional for the bride to adopt her husband's surname upon marriage, but she is not legally required to do so. If she chooses to take her husband's name, a deed poll is not required; the marriage certificate is sufficient documentary evidence to show that she has changed her surname. If she decides to retain her maiden name, she can adopt her husband's name at any time in the future without a deed poll. A groom has no such legal right to change his name.

A surname must be legally changed by deed poll:

* If the couple choose to have a double-barrelled or hyphenated surname.

* If the bride wishes to use her maiden name as a middle name and adopt her husband's surname.

If the bride wishes to change the surname of any children from a previous relationship to that of her new husband, this will also require a deed poll.

DOCUMENTATION

The marriage certificate is usually the only document needed to change names on official papers, identification and accounts, but sometimes a passport is also required. Additional copies of the certificate can be purchased from the Registrar of births, deaths and marriages at the local register office. The bride might find it useful to carry a copy or photocopy of the marriage certificate with her in the months following the wedding.

NAME CHANGE CHECKLIST

* Passport Office: the UK passport service will allow the passport to be altered up to three months prior to the wedding, but once it has been altered the bride cannot use her passport until she is married. Ensure that the name on the bride's honeymoon tickets corresponds with that on her passport as certain countries may refuse entry if this is not the case.

* DVLA: the DVLA requires the bride to send them original identity documents showing proof of her change of name, her photo card and its paper counterpart. There is no fee for the licence to be altered and the bride can drive while her licence is with the DVLA.

* Inland Revenue: the bride must inform the Inland Revenue of her name change using her National Insurance number as a reference.

* NHS and dentist: the bride should update her records with her GP. She will be issued with a new medical card; her NHS number will not change. She should also inform her dental surgery of the change. A GP can advise her on amending her details if she is registered for organ donation, or she can change her details online.

* Bank or building society: the bride can change the name on her account by visiting any branch of her bank or building society with her marriage certificate and amended passport. A name change will not affect any direct debits, but new cards will take approximately five days to be sent out. The bank might also pass on news of her name change to the credit bureaux to unify financial records under her maiden and married names. It is also necessary to contact all relevant mortgage, credit card, store card, insurance and utility companies.

* Clubs, societies, school and university alumni associations: a telephone call or letter after the wedding giving details of any name change should suffice. Many gyms or private members clubs wish to see new identification documents.

* Mobile phone account: take the relevant identification documents into the nearest network dealership.

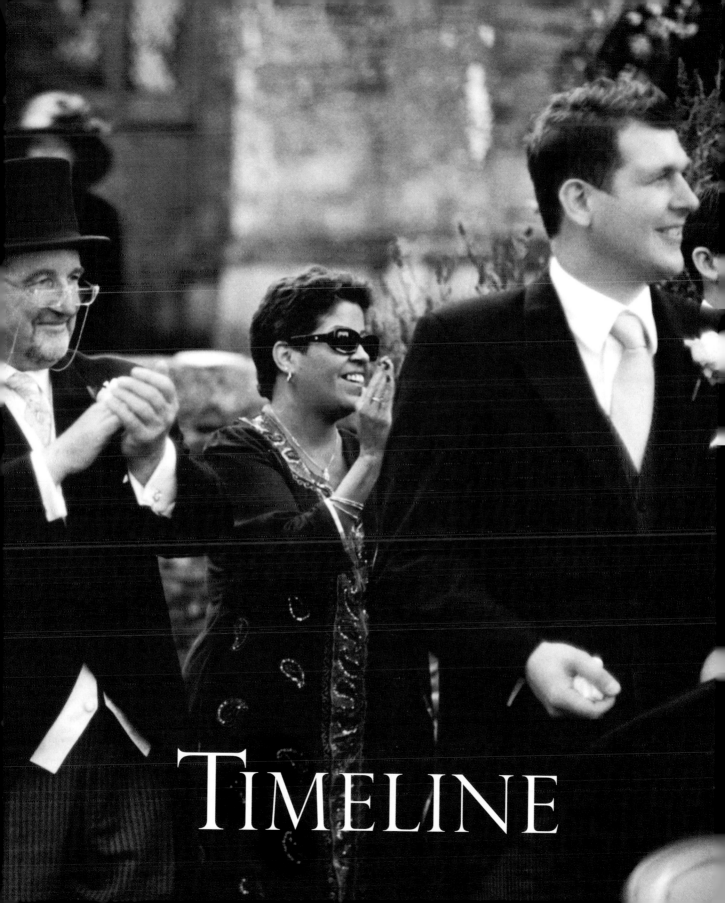

TIMELINE

9–12 Months Before

* Announce the engagement in newspapers.

* Choose a wedding planner (if required).

* Buy a wedding book or organiser and set up a filing system for details and receipts.

* Decide on the type of wedding: religious or civil.

* Meet religious minister/registrar to discuss ceremony.

* Arrange for families to meet (if necessary).

* Choose the wedding date.

* Set the budget.

* Organise responsibilities for family members.

* Choose and book venues for wedding and reception.

* Investigate photographers; an engagement photo can be taken at this point.

* Obtain menus and cost estimates from caterers.

* Purchase wedding insurance.

* Choose best man, bridesmaids, pageboys and ushers.

* Look into florists and check seasonal flowers.

* Make appointments to try on wedding dresses.

* Look into honeymoon ideas and destinations.

* Draw up a guest list.

* Decide whether children are to be invited.

6–9 Months Before

❈ Obtain a licence or marriage certificate and arrange banns or registrar's notice.

❈ Discuss the music with an organist, music group or wedding music company.

❈ Discuss readings with the minister or registrar.

❈ Ask family members or friends if they would like to read at the ceremony.

❈ Choose and confirm the caterers.

❈ See a wine merchant about wine and champagne.

❈ Order the wedding cake.

❈ Decide on a wedding-list company and register.

❈ Choose flowers for bouquets, buttonholes, the venue and table centres.

❈ Finalise the guest list.

❈ Design and order the invitations and envelopes.

❈ Look into the place cards, menus and seating plans.

❈ Decide who will print the order of service sheets.

❈ Book transport to and from the wedding venue for the bridal party and groom's party.

❈ Organise a car to the wedding-night hotel or airport.

❈ Book local hotel rooms or B&B for wedding party and close family.

❈ Book the honeymoon.

❈ Book time off work for the run-up to the wedding and the honeymoon.

❈ Confirm that the florist, photographer, DJ and/or other musical entertainment are all booked, with deposits paid.

❈ Reserve any extra sound equipment or furniture required for the reception.

❈ Book crèche facilities or child entertainers.

❈ Buy or order the wedding dress.

❈ Book make-up and hair stylists for a trial run and the wedding day.

❈ Look into bridal accessories – veil, shoes, underwear and cover-up.

3—6 Months Before

⚜ Consider save the date cards.

⚜ Hire or buy outfits for the groom's party, or inform them of the dress code.

⚜ Choose and order outfits for the bridesmaids.

⚜ Choose shoes, veil and other accessories for the bride and bridesmaids.

⚜ Gently spread the word among family and other guests about dress codes for men.

⚜ Choose, buy and insure wedding rings.

⚜ Choose the presents for the wedding list.

⚜ Choose presents for best man, ushers and attendants.

⚜ Order favours for the reception (if required).

⚜ Design orders of service and have them proof-checked by the minister or registrar.

⚜ Print orders of service (don't forget spares).

⚜ Send off the forms for the bride's new passport.

⚜ Investigate visas or inoculations for the honeymoon, and arrange if necessary.

⚜ The groom should organise a wedding-night hotel.

⚜ Plan enclosures for the invitation: maps, nearby B&Bs, wedding list information or no-children rules.

⚜ Plan pre- or post-wedding lunches (if required).

⚜ Confirm hen and stag party details.

1–3 Months Before

✳ Send out the wedding invitations.

✳ Keep a list of acceptances and refusals, and send out any extra invitations.

✳ Start the reception seating plan, but allow for changes.

✳ Set a rehearsal time with the minister or registrar and inform the wedding party.

✳ Confirm prices with suppliers, double-check delivery or arrival timings and pay any outstanding amounts.

✳ Meet the hair and make-up stylists to decide on a style for the bride and bridesmaids.

✳ Final dress fittings for bride and bridesmaids.

✳ Choose a first dance and consider practising.

✳ Send copies of readings to the readers for rehearsal.

✳ Buy clothes and accessories for the honeymoon.

✳ Order honeymoon currency/travellers' cheques and reconfirm honeymoon details.

✳ Check that visas, passports and jabs are all up to date.

✳ Handle any business and legal practicalities concerning name and address changes.

✳ Try on the full bridal outfit – including jewellery and lingerie – and practise walking in shoes.

✳ Pick up wedding rings; have them engraved, if desired.

✳ Have engagement ring cleaned or polished.

✳ Arrange who will pick up or wait for any deliveries on or before the day.

✳ Arrange safe storage at the reception venue for presents given on the day.

✳ Instruct reception staff to save flowers after reception.

✳ Make a note of favourite songs for the DJ or band.

✳ Politely chase any forgetful guests for RSVPs.

✳ Give caterers notice of special dietary requirements.

✳ Buy a guest book or photo album for guests to sign.

✳ Hold the hen and stag parties.

✳ Organise domestic arrangements for the honeymoon period: pets, house-sitting and so on.

1 Week Before

✼ Collect the wedding dress and bridesmaids' outfits.

✼ Practise putting on the wedding dress with whoever will be helping on the big day.

✼ Reconfirm all details with suppliers and staff involved on the day; this includes cakes, flowers, photographs, hair and make-up stylists.

✼ Make a list of telephone numbers in case of any emergencies on the day: local cab firms, the wedding party's mobiles, suppliers.

✼ Chase last minute RSVPs.

✼ Draw up the final seating plan.

✼ Make up extra copies of the seating plan for the caterer, photographer and best man.

✼ Divide place cards into envelopes for the caterers laying the tables, allowing one envelope per table.

✼ Confirm final numbers, dietary requirements and special requests with the caterers.

✼ Reconfirm all transport arrangements.

✼ Organise reserved seating for the ceremony and brief the ushers.

✼ Keep an eye on the weather forecast; make provision for extreme conditions, for example extra umbrellas, blankets, fans and bottles of water.

✼ Check the details for pre-/post-wedding lunch or the rehearsal dinner (if applicable).

✼ Pack and organise luggage for the honeymoon, including new passport.

✼ Brief the best man on final payments due on the day, and supply cash or cheques, as required.

✼ Draw up a list of important family and friends for the photographer, with a copy for the best man.

✼ Brief the best man and chief bridesmaid on any final logistics and last minute duties.

✼ Confirm individuals responsible for rental returns after the wedding.

✼ Check with the parents, minister/registrar, bridesmaids and ushers about the wedding rehearsal and other timings.

✼ The couple should spend some time together, and try to enjoy time with family and close friends.

Picture Credits

Acknowledgements

EDITORIAL CONSULTANT:

Lucy Attwood
www.lucyattwood.com

WEDDING PHOTOGRAPHY:

Victoria Dawe
www.victoriadawephotography.com

Dan Stevens
www.danstevens.co.uk

WEDDING ADVISORS:

Browns Brides
www.brownsfashion.com

The Designer Wedding Show
www.designerweddingshow.co.uk

McQueens
www.mcqueens.co.uk

Henry Poole & Co
www.henrypoole.com

Savoir Design
www.savoirdesign.co.uk

White Canvas Tents
www.whitecanvastents.com

The Wren Press
www.wrenpress.co.uk

Special thanks to Jean Egbunike, Ian Castello–Cortes,
Stephanie Molloy and Tom Bryant.

Debrett's would like to thank the couples whose
weddings feature in this book:

Adam and Claire Bonudy, Janey and Joby Burgess, Anna
and Paul Forsyth, Mary and Wesley Kent, Luke and Julie
Lloyd Davies, Lord and Lady Edward Manners, Dominic
and Elizabeth Plum, Sam and Juliet Rose, David and
Margie Slade, Chloe Mason and Tim van Someren,
Duncan and Alice Swinhoe, Karen and Oliver Ward.

Rachel Meddowes would like to thank Stuart Parvin,
Nick Laing, John Frieda, Adrienne Gignoux, Venetia and
Dave Curtis, Daniel Sandler, Nazli Arad, Robbie Honey,
Georgie Lancaster, Gill Christophers, Zelda Suite Pedlar,
Boyse Fry, Jan and Alex Meddowes, Rachel Mount, Tara
Goldsmid Patterson, Lucia Lindsay, Bridget Brown,
Alejandra Morales and Lauren Saunders.

Index

Where more than one page number is listed against a
heading, page numbers in bold indicate significant
treatment of a subject.